Poetic Diaries 1971 and 1972

Also by Eugenio Montale

POETRY

Ossi di seppia (Cuttlefish Bones)
Le occasioni (The Occasions)
La bufera e altro (The Storm and Other Things)
Quaderno di traduzioni (Notebook of Translations)
Satura (Miscellany)
Quaderno di quattro anni (Poetic Notebook 1974-1977)
Tutte le poesie (Collected Poems)
L'opera in versi (Poetical Works)
Altri versi e poesie disperse (Other and Uncollected Poems)
Diario postumo (Poshumous Diary)

PROSE

Farfalla di Dinard (Butterfly of Dinard)
Eugenio Montale/Italo Svevo: Lettere con gli scritti di Montale su Svevo
(The Montale-Svevo Letters, with Montale's Writings on Svevo)
Audo da fé: Cronache in due tempi (Act of Faith: Chronicles of Two Periods)
Fuori di casa (Away from Home)
La poesia non esiste (Poetry Doesn't Exist)
Nel nostro tempo (In Our Time)
Sulla poesia (On Poetry)
Lettere a Quasimodo (Letters to Quasimodo)
Prime alla Scala (Openings at la Scala)
Quaderno genovese (Genoa Notebook)
Lettere a Clizia (Letters to Clizia)

Also by the translator, William Arrowsmith

TRANSLATIONS

The Bacchae; Cyclops; Orestes; Hercuba; and *Heracles* by Euripides
Satyricon by Petronious
Birds by Aristophanes
Clouds by Aristophanes
Dialogues with Leucò by Cesare Pavese
(translated with D. S. Carne-Ross)
Alcestis by Euripides
Hard Labor by Cesare Pavese
That Bowling Alley on the Tiber by Michelangelo Antonioni
The Storm and Other Things by Eugenio Montale
The Occasions by Eugenio Montale
Cuttlefish Bones by Eugenio Montale
Satura by Eugenio Montale
The Collected Poems of Eugenio Montale: 1925–1977 by Eugenio Montale
Poetic Notebook 1974–1977 by Eugenio Montale

EDITORSHIPS

The Craft and Context of Translation (edited with Roger Shattuck)
Image of Italy
Six Modern Italian Novellas
The Greek Tragedies in New Translations
(in thirty-three volumes, in process of appearance)

Poetic Diaries
1971 and 1972

Eugenio Montale

Translated by William Arrowsmith

Introduction by Rosanna Warren

W. W. NORTON & COMPANY
New York   London

Poetic Diary: 1971, translation copyright © 2012 by Beth Arrowsmith, Nancy Arrowsmith, and Rosanna Warren.
Poetic Diary: 1972, translation copyright © 2012 by Beth Arrowsmith, Nancy Arrowsmith, and Rosanna Warren.
Diario del '71 e del '72, copyright © 1973 by Arnoldo Mondadori Editore S.p.A., Milano.

For information about permission to reproduce selections from this book, write to Permissions, W. W. Norton & Company, Inc., 500 Fifth Avenue, New York, NY 10110

For information about special discounts for bulk purchases, please contact W. W. Norton Special Sales at specialsales@wwnorton.com or 800-233-4830

Manufacturing by Courier Westford
Production manager: Louise Mattarelliano

Library of Congress Cataloging-in-Publication Data

Montale, Eugenio, 1896–1981.
[Diario del '71 e del '72. English]
Poetic diaries 1971 and 1972 / Eugenio Montale ; translated by William Arrowsmith ; introduction by Rosanna Warren.
   p. cm.
Includes bibliographical references and index.
ISBN 978-0-393-34419-6 (pbk.)
1. Montale, Eugenio, 1896–1981—Translations into English.
I. Arrowsmith, William, 1924–1992. II. Title.
PQ4829.O565A2 2012b
851'.912—dc23
            2012029599

W. W. Norton & Company, Inc.
500 Fifth Avenue, New York, N.Y. 10110
www.wwnorton.com

W. W. Norton & Company Ltd.
Castle House, 75/76 Wells Street, London W1T 3QT

1 2 3 4 5 6 7 8 9 0

Contents

Contents

Contents

Contents

Introduction

Eugenio Montale towers over Italian poetry in the twentieth century. Born in Genoa in 1896, he trained as an opera singer, fought briefly in the First World War as a second lieutenant, and returned home after the war to continue his intense self-education in art, literature, and philosophy. His first book of poems, *Ossi di seppia* (*Cuttlefish Bones*), appeared in 1925. The poems, evoking the rocky, sun-smashed Ligurian coast where the poet had spent most of his summers, startled readers with their harsh sounds and disruption of Italian conventions of magniloquence and lyricism. At the same time, they announced a not-so-discreet resistance to the Fascist ideology that was taking hold of Italy in this decade: "Don't ask me for formulas to open worlds / for you: all I have are gnarled syllables, / branch-dry. All I can tell you now is this: / What we are *not*, what we do *not* want" (from "Don't ask me for words . . . ").

Montale's second book of poems, *Le occasioni* (*The Occasions*), was published in 1939 as the world hurtled into war. By this time, Montale had moved to Florence where in 1929 he was appointed director of an important library, the Gabinetto Scientifico Letterario G. P. Vieusseux, a post from which he was fired in 1938 for refusing to join the Fascist party. The poems of *Le occasioni* are more concentrated and elliptical than those of *Ossi*, and they are dominated by a powerful Dantesque Muse called Clizia (after Ovid's nymph who was transformed into a sunflower by her love for the sun god, Apollo). The model for Clizia was the American Dante scholar Irma Brandeis, whom

Montale met at the Gabinetto Vieusseux and with whom he experienced an epiphanic passion. The lovers were separated by the Second World War, but the affair left its traces in much of *Le occasioni* and in many poems of Montale's third book, *La bufera e altro (The Storm and Other Things)*, published in 1956. The memory of Clizia haunted the poet until his death; see, for instance, "To C." in this volume. It is for her he wrote *Le occasioni*'s "Motets," one of the great erotic suites of the century. The romance is documented in a book published after Montale's death, *Lettere a Clizia*, edited by Rosanna Bettarini, Gloria Manghetti, and Franco Zabagli (Milan: Mondadori, 2006).

La bufera's title recalls the storm of passion whirling the lustful in Canto V of Dante's *Inferno* and the storm of world war. The poems depict, at times obliquely, the conditions of war and Fascist oppression: "then the hard crack, the castanets, the shaking / of tambourines over the thieving ditch, / the stamp of the fandango" ("The Storm"). They also extend the poet's vision of redemptive female figures; Clizia shares the book with a more overtly erotic presence, the Vixen. But by this time Montale had married the woman with whom he had lived throughout the war, Drusilla Tanzi Marangoni, neither an angel nor a vixen but a myopic, down-to-earth, ironic woman nicknamed Mosca (the Fly). Her death in 1963 inspired another majestic sequence of love poems, the "Xenia" elegies in Montale's fourth book, *Satura* (1971).

Satura shocked its readers. It announced a radical shift in Montale's poetics: He banished the lushness of his earlier landscapes and seascapes and the Dantesque/Petrarchan allusive richness of the earlier love poems, and presented downright anti-lyrical work. He wanted, he said in an interview, to attain "the dimension of a poetry that seems to incline toward prose and at the same time refuses it."* The poems of *Satura* (whose

---

*Forti, 85.

Latin title suggests satire but also means "a mixed dish, a stew of different styles") seem journalistic, diaristic, anecdotal, and caustic. Reading them required a new aesthetics and a new critical language to account for this poetry built on declaration and juxtaposition rather than on metaphor and melody.

Montale extended this abrasive style into the poems of this volume, *Diario del '71 e del '72 (Poetic Diaries 1971 and 1972)*, published in 1973. It would be a mistake to take the title literally and to regard these poems as diary jottings. They are no more such haphazard entries than the poems of *Le occasioni* were "occasional." A brusque economy rules them and their strategies of presenting image, situation, and incident. Apparently casual, their observations—highly selected—expand into symbol: the garbage strike in "The Triumph of Trash" points to a metaphysical condition; the old clock in "The Chiming Pendulum Clock" prefigures the winding down of all life ("I, who was once Time, renounce time"); the old turtle missing a leg seems an image of the aged poet or any elderly person reliving his sorrows: "To the tortoise, all ages are one, all lesions / contemporary" ("In an 'Italian' Garden").

From the first poem, "To Leone Traverso," the collection meditates obsessively on the condition of its own art, partly in poems about music and painting, partly in arguments about language. Addressing his friend Traverso, an erudite, idealistic scholar and classicist, the poet presents himself, by contrast, as a disenchanted spoiler: "My clumsy fingers / fumble the celeste or the mallets / of the vibraphone, but the music always / eludes me. And, anyway, music / of the spheres it never was." In "Poor Art," the poet (who also painted) describes his paintings as humiliated objects composed of dregs. Yet this art made of leavings, ash, and flecks of toothpaste has its own eloquence and powers of survival, as the concluding lines, addressed to the dead Mosca, say forcefully: "It's this part of me that manages to survive / the nothingness that was in me, the whole that you / unwittingly, were." (The art hidden in these deceptively prosy lines derives from classical rhetoric; Arrowsmith catches the curt antithesis and parallelism of Montale's Italian: nothingness/whole; was in me / you were.)

A poetry of disillusionment; a poetry critical of the hedonistic and corrupt postwar culture it observes; a poetry pondering its own making as a kind of stammering: no wonder that in his deeply Catholic and also worldly country Montale finds himself questioning philosophical and religious transcendence. "I've never seen Him," snaps the speaker of "Like Zaccheus." "It's Pentecost, and there's no way / tongues of fire can descend from heaven," declares "Fire." "I don't know where he is, the Lord of the Revels, / Ruler of the world and the other spheres," complains the speaker in "The Lord of the Revels." The book as a whole builds up a negative theology of language; only a consciousness dogged by ideas of the sacred and of human nobility would raise such questions, or snarl and mourn at the absences perceived. For this desolate predicament, Montale invented his punished language, the reduced music of his late years. The Muse who presides, once proud and tall, now dresses like a scarecrow: "She still has / one sleeve, with which she conducts her scrannel / straw quartet. It's the only music I can stand" ("My Muse").

Rosanna Warren

Editor's Note

The classicist William Arrowsmith spent the fiercest energy of his last years translating the poetry of Eugenio Montale. His translations of Montale are poetic re-creations of a high order, reflecting Arrowsmith's lifelong devotion to the art and his particular devotion to the art of Montale. He elucidated the poems not only in his idiomatic, surging versions, ever alert to the pull and swerve of the original, but also in his monumental notes, which by themselves constitute a generous body of criticism and a profound engagement with Montale's aesthetics. Arrowsmith received the International Eugenio Montale Prize in Parma in 1990.

When Arrowsmith died in 1992, he left in manuscript his translations of every volume of poetry by Eugenio Montale arranged by the poet himself, except for *The Storm and Other Things* (*La bufera e altro*) and *The Occasions* (*Le occasioni*), which had already appeared from W. W. Norton in W.A.'s translation. *Altri versi*, put together for Montale by Giorgio Zampa and published a few months before the poet's death in 1981, was not included; nor, for obvious reasons, was *Diario postumo*, edited by Annalisa Cima and not published in toto until 1996. In 1992, Norton brought out, in a posthumous publication, W.A.'s translation of Montale's *Cuttlefish Bones* (*Ossi di seppia*), and in 1998 his translation of *Satura*.

This translation of *Poetic Diaries 1971 and 1972* also appeared in *The Collected Poems of Eugenio Montale 1925–1977* (W. W. Norton, 2012). I have added notes to aid comprehension, but have made no attempt to supply the full interpretative context W.A. would have provided had he lived. I abbreviate Montale to E.M., and Marco Forti, *Per conoscere Montale* (Milan: Mondadori, 1976), to Forti. Francesca Ricci's *Guida alla lettura di Montale: Diario del '71 e del '72* (Rome: Carocci, 2005) has been especially helpful; I abbreviate it to Ricci.

In preparing this book for publication, I have relied on the invaluable assistance of Alex Effgen of the Boston University Editorial Institute and Liza Katz who exercised great ingenuity in transforming paper manuscript pages into digital text. I am also grateful to Jill Bialosky for her faith in Montale and in William Arrowsmith and her determination to produce this book; to Lucio Mariani, Michael Putnam, Peter Schwartz, Alan Smith, and Rebecca West for help with the notes; and to Beth and Nancy Arrowsmith, William Arrowsmith's daughters, for their gracious support at every step along the way.

R.W.

Poetic Diary:
1971

A Leone Traverso

I

Quando l'indiavolata gioca a nascondino
difficile acciuffarla per il toupet.
E non vale lasciarsi andare sulla corrente
come il neoterista Goethe sperimentò.
Muffiti in-folio con legacci e borchie
non si confanno, o raro, alle sue voglie.
Pure tu l'incontrasti, Leone, la poesia
in tutte le sue vie, tu intarmolito
sì, ma rapito sempre e poi bruciato
dalla vita.

II

Sognai anch'io di essere un giorno mestre
de gay saber; e fu speranza vana.
Un lauro risecchito non dà foglie
neppure per l'arrosto. Con maldestre
dita sulla celesta, sui pestelli
del vibrafono tento, ma la musica
sempre più s'allontana. E poi non era
musica delle Sfere . . . Mai fu gaio
né savio né celeste il mio sapere.

2

To Leone Traverso

I

When the wild Witch plays hide-and-seek,
catching her by the forelock is tricky work.

And it's no good, just going with the flow,
as experimental Goethe did.

Moldy folios with ties and bosses
only rarely fit her fancies.

Poetry in all her forms—
you faced her down, Leone—you, motheaten,
yes, but always ravished by life and by it
at last consumed.

II

I too once dreamed of being *mestre
de gay saber;* to no avail.
A withered bay-tree sprouts no leaves,
not even for the roast. My clumsy fingers
fumble the celeste or the mallets
of the vibraphone, but the music always
eludes me. And, anyway, music
of the spheres it never was . . . What I knew
was never gay, or wise, or heavenly.

L'arte povera

La pittura
da cavalletto costa sacrifizi
a chi la fa ed è sempre un sovrappiù
per chi la compra e non sa dove appenderla.
Per qualche anno ho dipinto solo ròccoli
con uccelli insaccati,
su carta blu da zucchero o cannelé da imballo.
Vino e caffè, tracce di dentifricio
se in fondo c'era un mare infiocchettabile,
queste le tinte.
Composi anche con cenere e con fondi
di cappuccino a Sainte-Adresse là dove
Jongkind trovò le sue gelide luci
e il pacco fu protetto da cellofane e canfora
(con scarso esito).
È la parte di me che riesce a sopravvivere
del nulla ch'era in me, del tutto ch'eri
tu, inconsapevole.

Poor Art

Easel
painting demands sacrifice
from the painter, even more from the man who buys it
and hasn't a clue where to hang it.
For several years all I painted was bird-traps—
birds snared in paper bags,
blue sugar-boxes or tubes of wrapping-paper.
If the background was a whitecapped sea,
my colors were wine, coffee, and flecks
of toothpaste.
I also composed with ashes and cappuccino
dregs at Sainte-Adresse, the place
where Jongkind found his icy lights,
and my package was protected by cellophane
and camphor (with no great success).
It's this part of me that manages to survive
the nothingness that was in me, the whole that you,
unwittingly, were.

Trascolorando

Prese la vita col cucchiaio piccolo
essendo
onninamente *fuori* e imprendibile.

Una ragazza imbarazzata, presto
sposa di un nulla vero
e imperfettibile.

Ebbe un altro marito che le dette
uno status
e la portò nel Libano quale utile
suo nécessaire da viaggio.

Ma lei rimpianse l'agenzia turistica
dove la trovò un tale
non meno selenita ma comprensibile.

Fu nello spazio tra i suoi due mariti,
una prenotazione per l'aereo e
bastò qualche parola.

L'uomo la riportava al suo linguaggio
paterno, succulento
e non chiese nemmeno quel che ebbe.

Nel Libano si vive come se il mondo
non esistesse, quasi
più sepolti dei cedri sotto la neve.

Changing Color

She took life with a demitasse spoon
being
utterly *out of it*, unseizable.

A confused girl, married young
to a real, unredeemable
nobody.

She had a second husband who gave her
a status
and took her to Lebanon as a convenient
overnight kit.

But she missed the travel agency
where another man found her, no less loony
but understandable.

It was in the interval between her two husbands;
all it took was a plane reservation
and a few brief words.

The man carried her off to his succulent
ancestral language
and didn't even inquire about hers.

In Lebanon people live as though the world
didn't exist, almost more buried
than cedars under the snow.

Lei lo ricorda in varie lingue, un barbaro
cocktail di impresti,
lui la suppone arabizzata, docile
ai festini e ai dileggi dei Celesti.

Lui si rivede pièfelpato, prono
sui tappeti di innumeri moschee
e il suo sguardo s'accende

delle pietre che mutano colore,
le alessandriti, le camaleontiche
da lei ora acquistate a poco prezzo
nei bazar.

Ma lei non ebbe prezzo, né lui stesso
quando cercava un'agenzia turistica
presso il Marble Arch.

Era un uomo affittabile, sprovvisto
di predicati,
pronto a riceverne uno. Ora che l'ha
pensa che basti. E lei? Felicemente

si ignora. Chi dà luce rischia il buio.

She recalls him in several languages, a barbarous
cocktail of borrowings,
he thinks her Arabized, docile
at the feasts and gibes of the Celestials.

He sees himself in slippers, prone
on the carpets of innumerable mosques,
and his gaze illumined

by stones of changing color,
alexandrites, chameleonites
newly acquired by her at bargain prices
in the bazaars.

But she had no price, nor did he
when he went searching for a travel agency
near Marble Arch.

He was a man-for-rent, devoid
of predicates,
ready to receive one. Now that he has one
he thinks it's enough. And she? Luckily

she doesn't know. Those who give light
risk the darkness.

Come Zaccheo

Si tratta di arrampicarsi sul sicomoro
per vedere il Signore se mai passi.
Ahimè, non sono un rampicante ed anche
stando in punta di piedi non l'ho mai visto.

Like Zaccheus

The problem's climbing the sycamore
to see if maybe the Lord is going by.
Alas, I'm no treecreeper, and even on tiptoes
I've never seen Him.

Il positivo

Prosterniamoci quando sorge il sole
e si volga ciascuno alla sua Mecca.
Se qualcosa ci resta, appena un sì
diciamolo, anche se con occhi chiusi.

The Positive

Let's salaam at sunrise,
let everyone turn toward his private Mecca.
If anything is left us, a bare Yes,
let's say it, though with eyes closed.

Il negativo

Tuorli d'un solo uovo entrano i giovani
nelle palestre della vita. Venere
li conduce, Mercurio li divide,
Marte farà il resto. Non a lungo
brillerà qualche luce sulle Acropoli
di questa primavera ancora timida.

The Negative

Young men, yolks of a single egg, stride
into the wrestling-ring of life. Venus
guides them, Mercury divides them,
Mars will finish matters. The scarce light
of this still shy spring won't shine for long
on the Acropolis.

A C.

Tentammo un giorno di trovare un modus
moriendi che non fosse il suicidio
né la sopravvivenza. Altri ne prese
per noi l'iniziativa; e ora è tardi
per rituffarci dallo scoglio.
Che un'anima malviva
fosse la vita stessa nel suo diapason
non lo credesti mai: le ore incalzavano,
a te bastò l'orgoglio, a me la nicchia
dell'imbeccatore.

To C.

We tried one day to find a *modus
moriendi* that wasn't suicide
or survival. Others took
the initiative for us, and now it's too late
for diving off the cliff again.
You never believed
a damaged spirit could be life itself
in its diapason: time
was rushing past, pride
sufficed for you, and I had my niche
as a feeder of birds.

Corso Dogali

Se frugo addietro fino a corso Dogali
non vedo che il Carubba con l'organino
a manovella
e il cieco che vendeva il bollettino
del lotto. Gesti e strida erano pari.
Tutti e due storpi ispidi rognosi
come i cani bastardi dei gitani
e tutti e due famosi nella strada,
perfetti nell'anchilosi e nei suoni.
La perfezione: quella che se dico
Carubba è il cielo che non ho mai toccato.

Corso Dogali

If I rummage back in time to Corso Dogali,
all I see is Carubba with his little
hand-cranked barrel-organ
and the blind man who peddled lottery
tickets. The identical gestures and shouts.
Both of them crippled, unshaven, scruffy
as the gypsies' mongrel curs,
and both notorious along the street,
perfect paralysis, perfect noise.
Perfection: when I say that word,
Carubba's the heaven I never touched.

Rosso su rosso

È quasi primavera e già i corimbi
salgono alla finestra che dà sul cortile.
Sarà presto un assedio di foglie e di formiche.
Un coleottero tenta di attraversare il libretto
delle mie Imposte Dirette, rosso su rosso.
Magari
potesse stingere anche sul contenuto. È suonato
il mezzogiorno, trilla qualche telefono
e una radio borbotta duecento morti
sull'autostrada, il record della Pasquetta.

Red on Red

It's almost spring and already clusters of flowers
are climbing up to the window overlooking
the courtyard. Soon there'll be a siege
of leaves and ants. A ladybug tries crossing
my income tax return: red on red. If only
she could efface the contents! The noon bell
has struck, telephones are jangling,
and a radio's droning on
about two hundred people killed on the highways,
a record for Easter.

Verso il fondo

La rete
che strascica sul fondo
non prende
che pesci piccoli.

Con altre reti ho preso
pesci rondine
e anche una testuggine
ma era morta.

Ora che mi riprovo
con amo e spago
l'esca rimane intatta
nell'acqua torbida.

Troppo spessore è intorno
di su, di giù nell'aria.
Non si procede: muoversi
è uno strappo.

Toward the Bottom

The net
that drags the bottom
pulls in
only small fry.

With other nets I've caught
flying gurnards
even a turtle
but he was dead.

Now that I try again
with hook and line
the bait dangles untouched
in the murky water.

Thickness on all sides,
up, down, in the air, too much.
Walking stops; movement's
a wrench.

Il Re pescatore

Si ritiene
che il Re dei pescatori non cerchi altro
che anime.

Io ne ho visto più d'uno
portare sulla melma delle gore
lampi di lapislazzulo.

Il suo regno è a misura di millimetro,
la sua freccia imprendibile
dai flash.

Solo il Re pescatore
ha una giusta misura,
gli altri hanno appena un'anima
e la paura
di perderla.

The Kingfisher

People hold
that the Fisher-King seeks only
souls.

I've seen more than one
dazzle slimy ponds with a blaze
of lapis lazuli.

His kingdom is measured in millimeters,
his invisible arrow
by its flashing.

Only the Kingfisher's
measure is right,
others hardly have souls
and dread
losing them.

Nel cortile

Nell'accidiosa primavera quando le ferie incombono
la città si svuota.
È dalle Idi di marzo che un vecchio merlo si posa
sul davanzale a beccare chichi di riso e briciole.
Non utile per lui scendere nel cortile
ingombro di tante macchine casse sacchi racchette.
Alla finestra di fronte un antiquario in vestaglia
e due gattini siamesi. Da un altro osservatorio
un ragazzino rossiccio che tira ai piccioni col flòbert.
Vasto l'appartamento del grande Oncologo,
sempre deserto e buio. Ma non fu tale una notte,
quando avvampò di luci alla notizia
che il prefato era accolto in parlamento.
Tanti gli stappamenti di sciampagna,
i flash, le risa, gli urli dei gratulanti
che anche la Gina fu destata e corse
tutta eccitata a dirmi: ce l'ha fatta!

In the Courtyard

In the torpid spring when the holidays loom,
the city empties.
Since the Ides of March, an old blackbird
has been perching on the window-sill, pecking
at breadcrumbs and grains of rice. No point
in fluttering down to the courtyard
crammed with all those cars, trunks, bags,
and tennis rackets. At the window opposite
an antiquarian in a dressing gown, and two
Siamese kittens. From another vantage
a red-faced boy with a beebee gun
is peppering pigeons. The huge apartment
of the great Oncologist is dark, deserted
as always. But one night things were different:
the place was ablaze with light at the news
the aforementioned had been elected to parliament.
Magnums of champagne were being uncorked,
flash-bulbs flaring, so much laughing,
such shrieks of congratulation that even Gina
woke up and ran in, all flustered, to tell me:
He made it!

I nascondigli

Quando non sono certo di essere vivo
la certezza è a due passi ma costa pena
ritrovarli gli oggetti, una pipa, il cagnuccio
di legno di mia moglie, un necrologio
del fratello di lei, tre o quattro occhiali
di lei ancora!, un tappo di bottiglia
che colpì la sua fronte in un lontano
cotillon di capodanno a Sils Maria
e altre carabattole. Mutano alloggio, entrano
nei buchi più nascosti, ad ogni ora
hanno rischiato il secchio della spazzatura.
Complottando tra loro si sono organizzati
per sostenermi, sanno più di me
il filo che li lega a chi vorrebbe
e non osa disfarsene. Più prossimo
negli anni il Gubelin automatico tenta
di aggregarvisi, sempre rifiutato.
Lo comprammo a Lucerna e lei disse
piove troppo a Lucerna non funzionerà mai.
E infatti . . .

Hiding Places

When I'm not sure I'm alive,
certainty's a few steps away. But it's painful
recovering objects—a pipe, my wife's
little wooden dog, her brother's obituary,
three or four pairs of her glasses,
the champagne cork that hit her on the forehead
at the New Year's cotillion years ago at Sils Maria,
and other kickshaws. They change lodgings, slip
into out-of-the-way crannies, constantly
in danger of being chucked into the trash.
They've hatched a plot, banding together
to save me; they know better than I
that a thread binds them to someone
who'd like to throw them out, but doesn't dare.
More recently the fancy quartz watch tried
to join the plot, but it always gets rejected.
We bought it at Lucerne and she said
there's too much rain in Lucerne, it'll
never work. And in fact . . .

El Desdichado

Sto seguendo sul video la Carmen di Karajan
disossata con cura, troppo amabile.

Buste color mattone, gonfie, in pila sul tavolo
imprigionano urla e lamentazioni.

Col paralume mobile vi ho gettato
solo un guizzo di luce, poi ho spento.

Non attendete da me pianto o soccorso fratelli.
Potessi mettermi in coda tra voi chiederei l'elemosina

di una parola che non potete darmi
perché voi conoscete soltanto il grido,

un grido che si spunta
in un'aria infeltrita, vi si aggiunge

e non parla.

El Desdichado

I'm watching Karajan's *Carmen* on TV,
scrupulously deboned, too *amabile*.

Brick-red envelopes, stuffed, piled on the table,
seal in shouts and lamentation.

Angling the lampshade, I lit them up
with a flash of light, then turned it off.

Don't expect sorrow or help from me, brothers.
If I could join your ranks, I'd beg for the alms

of a word you can't give me
since all you know is the scream,

a scream muffled in an air
like felt, that blends into it

and doesn't speak.

Retrocedendo

Il tarlo è nato, credo, dentro uno stipo
che ho salvato da sgombri e inondazioni.
Il suo traforo è lentissimo, il microsuono non cessa.
Da mesi probabilmente si nutre del pulviscolo
frutto del suo lavoro. Si direbbe che ignori
la mia esistenza, io non la sua. Io stesso
sto trivellando a mia insaputa un ceppo
che non conosco e che qualcuno osserva
infastidito dal cri cri che n'esce,
un qualcuno che tarla inconsapevole
del suo tarlante e così via in un lungo
cannocchiale di pezzi uno nell'altro.

Receding

I think the woodworm was born in a chest
I'd saved from various moves and floods.
He tunnels very slowly, his mini-shrilling never stops.
For months he's probably fed himself on the dusty fruits
of his labor. You might say he's unaware
of my existence, but I'm aware of his. Fact is
I've unknowingly been tunnelling away myself
in an unfamiliar log which someone, annoyed
by the cries coming from it, is watching—
a someone who's boring away in turn, unconscious
of his own boring, and so on, inside a long telescope,
each tube fitted inside another.

La mia Musa

La mia Musa è lontana: si direbbe
(è il pensiero dei più) che mai sia esistita.
Se pure una ne fu, indossa i panni dello spaventacchio
alzato a malapena su una scacchiera di viti.

Sventola come può; ha resistito a monsoni
restando ritta, solo un po' ingobbita.
Se il vento cala sa agitarsi ancora
quasi a dirmi cammina non temere,
finché potrò vederti ti darò vita.

La mia Musa ha lasciato da tempo un ripostiglio
di sartorial teatrale; ed era d'alto bordo
chi di lei si vestiva. Un giorno fu riempita
di me e ne andò fiera. Ora ha ancora una manica
e con quella dirige un suo quartetto
di cannucce. È la sola musica che sopporto.

My Muse

My Muse is distant: one might say
(and most have thought it) that she never existed.
But if she was my Muse, she's dressed like a scarecrow
awkwardly propped on a checkerboard of vines.

She flaps as best she can; she's withstood monsoons
without falling, though she sags a little.
When the wind dies, she keeps on fluttering
as though telling me: Go on, don't be afraid,
as long as I can see you, I'll give you life.

My Muse long since left a store room
full of theatrical outfits, and an actor costumed by her
was an actor with class. Once, she was filled
with me and she walked proud and tall. She still has
one sleeve, with which she conducts her scrannel
straw quartet. It's the only music I can stand.

Il tuffatore

Il tuffatore preso au ralenti
disegna un arabesco ragniforme
e in quella cifra forse si identifica
la sua vita. Chi sta sul trampolino
è ancora morto, morto chi ritorna
a nuoto alla scaletta dopo il tuffo,
morto chi lo fotografa, mai nato
chi celebra l'impresa.
                    Ed è poi vivo
lo spazio di cui vive ogni movente?
Pietà per le pupille, per l'obiettivo,
pietà per tutto che si manifesta,
pietà per il partente e per chi arriva,
pietà per chi raggiunge o ha raggiunto,
pietà per chi non sa che il nulla e il tutto
sono due veli dell'Impronunciabile,
pietà per chi lo sa, per chi lo dice,
per chi lo ignora e brancola nel buio
delle parole!

The Diver

The diver photographed *au ralenti*
cuts a spider arabesque
and maybe that figure is identical
with his life. The man standing on the diving-board
is dead again, the swimmer going
back to the board after diving is dead,
the photographer's dead, the man applauding the event
was never born.
                    And so? Is it alive—
the space filled by every living thing?
Pity for the eyes, for the objective,
pity for everything that appears,
pity for those leaving and those arriving,
pity for those who achieve or have achieved,
pity for those who know that all and nothing
are two veils of the Unpronounceable,
pity for those who know it, for those who say it,
for those who don't know it and grope
in the darkness of words!

Dove comincia la carità

Questa violenta raffica di carità
che si abate su noi
è un'ultima impostura.

Non sarà mai ch'essa cominci *at home*
come ci hanno insegnato alla Berlitz; mai
accadrà che si trovi nei libri di lettura.

E non certo da te, Malvolio, o dalla tua banda,
non da ululi di tromba, non da chi ne fa
una seconda pelle che poi si butta via.

Non appartiene a nessuno la carità. Sua pari
la bolla di sapone che brilla un attimo, scoppia,
e non sa di chi era il soffio.

Where Charity Begins

This violent squall of charity
beating down upon us
is a final imposition.

It will never begin "at home,"
as they taught us at Berlitz; it will never
be found in children's primers.

And certainly not by you, Malvolio, or your gang,
not by blaring bugles, nor by those who use it
as a second skin and then slough it.

Charity belongs to nobody. Its image,
a soap-bubble, shines for an instant, bursts,
and never knows who blew it.

Il pirla

Prima di chiudere gli occhi mi hai detto pirla,
una parola gergale non traducibile.
Da allora me la porto addosso come un marchio
che resiste alla pomice. Ci sono anche altri
pirla nel mondo ma come riconoscerli?
I pirla non sanno di esserlo. Se pure
ne fossero informati tenterebbero
di scollarsi con le unghie quello stimma.

The Prick

Before dozing off you called me a prick,
a vulgarism not easily unpacked.
Since then I wear it like a brand
no pumice could remove. There are other
pricks around, but how can we spot them?
Pricks don't know they're pricks.
If they did, they'd use their nails
and try to gouge that stigma out.

Il fuoco

Siamo alla Pentecoste e non c'è modo
che scendano dal cielo lingue di fuoco.
Eppure un Geremia apparso sul video
aveva detto che ormai sarà questione di poco.
Di fuoco non si vede nulla, solo
qualche bombetta fumogena all'angolo di via Bigli.
Questi farneticanti in doppiopetto o in sottana
non sembrano molto informati del loro mortifero aspetto.
Il fuoco non viene dall'alto ma dal basso,
non s'è mai spento, non è mai cresciuto,
nessuno l'ha mai veduto, fuochista o vulcanologo.
Chi se ne accorge non dà l'allarme, resta muto.
Gli uccelli di malaugurio non sono più creduti.

Fire

It's Pentecost, and there's no way
tongues of fire can descend from heaven.
Still, some T.V. Jeremiah
said it could happen any day.
There's no sign of fire, only
a couple of smoke-bombs at the corner
of Via Bigli. These madmen in double-breasted
suits or cassocks don't really seem aware
of their lethal look. Fire
doesn't come from above but below;
it's never been put out, never spread;
nobody, neither fireman nor vulcanologist,
has ever seen it. Those who do
don't call for help, they keep quiet.
Birds of ill-omen lack credibility these days.

A quella che legge i giornali

Tra sprazzi di sole e piovaschi
non ci si orienta sul tempo.
C'è poco baccano fuori,
il canarino non canta.
Gli hanno portato una moglie
e lui non apre più il becco.
Il tempo sembra indeciso
sulla sua stessa funzione.
Dobbiamo farci coraggio,
non è arrivata la posta,
non sono usciti i giornali,
non c'è tant'altro ma basta
per inceppare la marcia.
Fermata del tutto non è
ma certo zoppica. Ecco
quello che conta. Star fermi,
attendere e non rallegrarsi
se l'ingranaggio perde i colpi.
Riprenderà non diverso,
meglio lubrificato
o peggio ma quello che importa
è non lasciarci le dita.
Solo le cripte, le buche,
i ricettacoli, solo
questo oggi vale, mia cara,
tu che non leggi e non ascolti, tu
. . . .
che leggi appena i giornali.

To That Woman Who Reads the Newspapers

Between splashes of sunlight and showers
we can't get our bearings on the times.
Outdoors there's no great commotion,
the male canary isn't singing.
They brought him a wife
and he no longer opens his beak.
Time in its very function
seems undecided.
We ought to feel encouraged:
the mail hasn't arrived,
the papers haven't been delivered,
there's not much else but still enough
to make the motor falter.
Time hasn't stopped completely
but it's clearly crippled. And that's
what counts. Keeping still,
listening, not rejoicing
when the timing-gear misses. Time
will crank up as usual, better lubricated
or worse, but what counts
is not losing our fingers.
Only crypts, holes,
hideouts—that's all
that matters today, my dear,
you who don't read and who don't listen, you
. . . .
who barely read the papers.

Il tiro a volo

Mi chiedi perché navigo
nell'insicurezza e non tento
un'altra rotta? Domandalo
all'uccello che vola illeso
perché il tiro era lungo e troppo larga
la rosa della botta.

Anche per noi non alati
esistono rarefazioni
non più di piombo ma di atti,
non più di atmosfera ma di urti.
Se ci salva una perdita di peso
è da vedersi.

Shooting at a Moving Target

You ask me why I sail
with no destination instead of trying
a different course? Ask
the bird soaring by unhurt
because it was a long shot and the caliber
too large.

Even for us wingless creatures
there are rarefactions,
not of lead but of acts,
not of atmosphere but shocks.
Whether loss of weight could save us
is moot.

Il rondone

Il rondone raccolto sul marciapiede
aveva le ali ingrommate di catrame,
non poteva volare.
Gina che lo curò sciolse quei grumi
con batuffoli d'olio e di profumi,
gli pettinò le penne, lo nascose
in un cestino appena sufficiente
a farlo respirare.
Lui la guardava quasi riconoscente
da un occhio solo. L'altro non si apriva.
Poi gradì mezza foglia di lattuga
e due chicchi di riso. Dormì a lungo.
Il giorno dopo all'alba riprese il volo
senza salutare.
Lo vide la cameriera del piano di sopra.
Che fretta aveva fu il commento. E dire
che l'abbiamo salvato dai gatti. Ma ora forse
potrà cavarsela.

The Swift

The swift crumpled on the sidewalk
had wings so daubed with tar
he couldn't fly.
Gina, who nursed him, loosened the gobs
with wads of cotton soaked in oil and perfume,
fluffed his feathers, and tucked him
in a little basket barely big enough
for him to breathe.
From one eye—the other eye was closed—
he peeped at her almost gratefully.
Later he accepted half a leaf of lettuce,
a few grains of rice, and a long nap.
At dawn the next day he flew away
without so much as a chirp.
The maid in the apartment upstairs saw him go.
What a rush was her comment. And to think
we'd saved him from the cats! But now maybe
he can wing it on his own.

La forma del mondo

Se il mondo ha la struttura del linguaggio
e il linguaggio ha la forma della mente
la mente con i suoi pieni e i suoi vuoti
è niente o quasi e non ci rassicura.

Così parlò Papirio. Era già scuro
e pioveva. Mettiamoci al sicuro
disse e affrettò il passo senza accorgersi
che il suo era il linguaggio del delirio.

The Form of the World

If the world is structured like language
and language is structured like the mind,
then the mind with its fullnesses and voids
is nothing, or almost, which isn't reassuring.

So said Papirius. It was already dark,
and raining. Let's find a safer spot,
he said, and hurried off, unaware
that he was talking the language of madness.

Il lago di Annecy

Non so perché il mio ricordo ti lega
al lago di Annecy
che visitai qualche anno prima della tua morte.
Ma allora non ti ricordai, ero giovane
e mi credevo padrone della mia sorte.
Perché può scattar fuori una memoria
così insabbiata non lo so; tu stessa
m'hai certo seppellito e non l'hai saputo.
Ora risorgi viva e non ci sei. Potevo
chiedere allora del tuo pensionato,
vedere uscirne le fanciulle in fila,
trovare un tuo pensiero di quando eri
viva e non l'ho pensato. Ora ch'è inutile
mi basta la fotografia del lago.

Lac d'Annécy

I don't know why my memory links you
to the Lac d'Annécy
which I visited a few years before you died.
But at the time I didn't remember you; I was young
and thought myself master of my fate.
How a memory so buried can suddenly erupt,
I don't know; you yourself certainly buried me
without ever knowing it. Now
you return to life and you're no longer there.
Once I could have asked about your boarding-school,
could have watched the little girls filing out,
could have discovered some thought of yours in those days
when you were still alive, and I didn't think of it.
Now that I can't, I'm content
with the photo of the lake.

Il poeta

Si bùccina che viva dando ad altri
la procura, la delega o non so che.
Pure qualcosa stringe tre le dita
il deputante, il deputato no.

Non gli hanno detto al bivio che doveva
scegliere tra due vite separate
e intersecanti mai. Lui non l'ha fatto.
È stato il Caso che anche se distratto
rimane a guardia dell'indivisibile.

The Poet

They trumpet that they live by giving others
their proxy, power of attorney, and whatever.
But it's the deputizer, not the deputy,
who presses something between his fingers.

They failed to tell him at the crossroads
that he had to choose between two separate,
never intersecting lives. He didn't choose.
It was left to Chance, however distracted,
to keep an eye on the indivisible.

Il grande affare

Quale sia il grande affare non s'è mai saputo.
Se la spinta del sangue o la deiezione
o la più pura forma dell'imbecillità.
Resta l'incerto stato del bastardume,
del mezzo e mezzo, del di tutto un po'.

Ma c'è un portento che mai fu voluto
da nessuno per sé, per altri sì.
Non fu opera d'uomo: lo dichiarano
i cani degli zingari, gli elìsei
mostri che ancora ringhiano qua e là.

The Big Deal

What the big deal was no one ever knew,
whether blood-rush or bowel movement
or the most undiluted idiocy.
What's left is bastard uncertainty,
half and half, a touch of everything.

But there's one portent nobody
ever wished on himself, only on others.
It wasn't the work of man: gypsy
dogs declare it, and those Elysian
monsters still snarling here and there.

Imitazione del tuono

Pare che ogni vivente
imiti un suo modello
ignorandolo, impresa improponibile.
Ma il peggio tocca a chi il suo
crede averlo davanti come una statua.
Non imitate il marmo, uomini. Se non potete
star fermi modellatevi sulla crusca,
sui capelli del vento, sulla raspa
delle cicale, sull'inverosimile
bubbolare del tuono a ciel sereno.
Modellatevi, dico, anche sul nulla
se v'illudete di potere ancora
rasentare la copia di quel pieno
che non è in voi!

Imitation of Thunder

It seems that every living thing
imitates its own model
by ignoring it, an impossible enterprise.
But the worst case is the man who thinks
his model stands before him like a statue.
Men, don't imitate marble.
If you can't stand still, model yourselves
on chaff, puffs of wind, the cicada's
rasping cry, the improbable
shudder of thunder from a cloudless sky.
Model yourselves, I say, even on nothing
if you deceive yourselves that you can still
make a fair copy of that fullness
you lack.

Al Congresso

Se l'uomo è l'inventore della vita
(senza di lui chi se n'accorgerebbe)
non ha l'uomo il diritto di distruggerla?

Tale al Congresso il detto dell'egregio
preopinante che mai mosse un dito
per uscire dal gregge.

At the Conference

If man is the inventor of life
(without him who'd notice it?)
doesn't he have the right to destroy it?

So he addressed the Conference—the distinguished
first speaker who had never lifted a finger
to distinguish himself from the crowd.

Il frullato

Allora
un salotto di stucchi
di mezzibusti e specchi
era la vita.
Il battito di un cuore
artificiale o vero
era poesia.
Scorribande di nuvole
non di streghe
erano un quadro,
la fistula il fischietto il campanaccio
dei bovi musica.
Ora c'è stata una decozione
di tutto in tutti e ognuno si domanda
se il frullino ch'è in opera nei crani
stia montando sozzura o zabaione.

Accorcia l'ultimo tuo straccio
Bernadette, beccafichi! ora che tutto oscilla
come il latte alla portoghese,
nessuno potrà dirti chi sei, chi eri,
se fosti viva o morta, se hai saputo
che il vero e il falso sono il retto e il verso
della stessa medaglia, accorcia, butta via,
non sostituire,
lasciati andare sulle tue creme,

The Milk-Shake

In those days
a living-room of stuccoes
busts and mirrors
was life.
The beating of a heart
imagined or real
was poetry.
Scurrying packs of clouds
not witches
were a painting;
panpipes, whistles, cow-bells
were music.
Now we've got a decoction
of everything in all and everyone wonders
whether the blender churning in his brain
is whipping up crap or zabaglione.

Cut off the last of your rags, Bernadette,
stuff yourself! Now that everything's a-quiver
like milk *alla portoghese*,
no one can tell you who you are,
or were, whether living or dead, whether you knew
that true and false were recto and verso
of the same coin—cut it off, throw it away,
no substitutes,
let yourself go, churn away at your creams,

a fondo non andrai,
c'è chi ti guarda e t'insegna
che quello che trema è il tic tac
di un orologio che non perderà
tanto presto la carica!

you'll never get to the bottom of things,
someone is watching you, teaching you
what's shaking is the tick-tock
of a wound-up watch that won't unwind
in a hurry!

Ne abbiamo abbastanza . . .

Ne abbiamo abbastanza di . . .
è ripetuto all'unanimità.
Ma di che poi? Della vita no
e della morte ohibò, non se ne parla.

Dal *di* comincia la biforcazione
della quale ogni ramo si biforca
per triforcarsi eccetera. Può darsi
che anche l'Oggetto sia
stanco di riprodursi.

We're fed up with . . .

We're fed up with . . .
Everyone repeats that phrase.
But fed up with what? Not life,
and death, ha! no one mentions that.

With that *with* bifurcation begins,
each branch bifurcating
in order to trifurcate, and so on. Maybe
even the Object is fed up
with reproducing itself.

La lingua di Dio

Se dio *è* il linguaggio, l'Uno che ne creò tanti altri
per poi confonderli
come faremo a interpellarlo e come
credere che ha parlato e parlerà
per sempre indecifrabile e questo è
meglio che nulla. Certo
meglio che nulla siamo
noi fermi alla balbuzie. E guai se un giorno
le voci si sciogliessero. Il linguaggio,
sia il nulla o non lo sia,
ha le sue astuzie.

The Language of God

If god *is* language, the One who created so many
in order to mingle them later,
how can we put our questions to him, how
believe that he's spoken, that he'll always
speak undecodably, and that this
is better than nothing? Clearly
it's better than nothing that we're stuck
with stammering. And woe to us if someday
the voices were all let loose. Language,
whether it's nothing or not,
has its wiles.

A questo punto

A questo punto smetti
dice l'ombra.
T'ho accompagnato in guerra e in pace e anche
nell'intermedio,
sono stata per te l'esaltazione e il tedio,
t'ho insufflato virtù che non possiedi,
vizi che non avevi. Se ora mi stacco
da te non avrai pena, sarai lieve
più delle foglie, mobile come il vento.
Devo alzare la maschera, io sono il tuo pensiero,
sono il tuo in-necessario, l'inutile tua scorza.
A questo punto smetti, stràppati dal mio fiato
e cammina nel cielo come un razzo.
C'è ancora qualche lume all'orizzonte
e chi lo vede non è un pazzo, è solo
un uomo e tu intendevi di non esserlo
per amore di un'ombra. T'ho ingannato
ma ora ti dico a questo punto smetti.
Il tuo peggio e il tuo meglio non t'appartengono
e per quello che avrai puoi fare a meno
di un'ombra. A questo punto
guarda con i tuoi occhi e anche senz'occhi.

At This Point

At this point, says the shadow,
stop.
In war and peace and in the interim too
I was at your side.
I was your boredom and your exaltation,
I inspired you with a virtue you don't possess,
with vices you didn't have. If I abandon you now,
you'll feel no pain, you'll be lighter
than leaves, supple as wind.
I must remove my mask, I'm your thought,
I'm your non-necessary, your useless husk.
At this point stop, free yourself of my breath,
rush rocket-like through the sky.
A few lights still shine on the horizon
and the man who sees them isn't mad, merely
a man, and, because you loved a shadow, you thought
you weren't a man. I've deceived you
but now I tell you: at this point, stop.
Your worst and your best are not your own,
and what will be yours someday, you can achieve
without a shadow. At this point
see with your own eyes, see without them too.

Se il male naturaliter non può smettere
non gli conviene il segno del negativo.

L'altro segno a chi tocca? È la domanda
che corre (anzi *non* corre affatto)
di bocca in bocca.

If evil *naturaliter* can't desist,
its minus sign serves no purpose.

Whose business is the plus? That's the question
running (or rather *not* running at all)
from mouth to mouth.

Non mi stanco di dire al mio allenatore
getta la spugna
ma lui non sente nulla perché sul ring o anche fuori
non s'è mai visto.
Forse, a suo modo, cerca di salvarmi
dal disonore. Che abbia tanta cura
di me, l'idiota, o io sia il suo buffone
tiene in bilico tra la gratitudine
e il furore.

I never tire of telling my trainer
throw in the sponge,
but he doesn't hear me since he's never
been seen in or even out of the ring.
Maybe, in his own way, he's trying
to save me from disgrace. That the idiot
cares so much for me, or I'm *his* fool,
keeps him wobbling between gratitude
and rage.

Il trionfo della spazzatura

Lo sciopero dei netturbini
può dare all'Urbe il volto che le conviene.
Si procede assai bene tra la lordura
se una Chantal piovuta qui dal nord
vi accoglierà con una sua forbita
grazia più chiara e nitida dei suoi cristalli.
Fuori le vecchie mura ostentano la miseria,
la gloria della loro sopravvivenza.
Lei stessa, la ragazza, difende meglio
la sua identità se per raggiungerla
ha circumnavigato isole e laghi
di vomiticcio e di materie plastiche.
Qui gli ospiti nemmeno si conoscono
tra loro, tutti incuriosi e assenti
da sé. Il trionfo della spazzatura
esalta chi non se ne cura, smussa
angoli e punte. Essere vivi e basta
non è impresa da poco. E lei pure,
lei che ci accoglie l'ha saputo prima
di tutti ed è una sua invenzione
non appresa dai libri ma dal dio senza nome
che dispensa la Grazia, non sa fare altro
ed è già troppo.

The Triumph of Trash

The garbage-collectors' strike
can provide the City with suitable features.
You maneuver quite adroitly through the garbage
when a Chantal, suddenly blowing in from the north,
welcomes you with one of her polished
graces, clearer and shinier than her goblets.
Outside, the old walls flaunt their suffering,
the glory of their survival.
She herself—the girl—is better able to shield
an identity won
by circumnavigating islands and lakes
of vomit and plastic trash.
Visitors here, full of curiosity and forgetful
of themselves, don't even know who's who.
The triumph of trash exalts those indifferent
to it, softening angles and points.
Being alive—just being alive—is no small
enterprise. And even she—the girl who welcomes us,
who knew all that before anyone else,
a discovery wholly her own, not acquired
from books but from the nameless god
who dispenses Grace—can't do otherwise,
which is enough, and more.

Il dottor Schweitzer

gettava pesci vivi a pellicani famelici.
Sono vita anche i pesci fu rilevato, ma
di gerarchia inferiore.

A quale gerarchia apparteniamo noi
e in quali fauci . . . ? Qui tacque il teologo
e si asciugò il sudore.

Dr. Schweitzer

threw live fish to starving pelicans.
Fish too, he pointed out, are a form of life, but
of lower order.

To what order do we belong, and in whose
jaws . . . ? Here the theologian broke off
and wiped away the sweat.

I primi di luglio

Siamo ai primi di luglio e già il pensiero
è entrato in moratoria.
Drammi non se ne vedono,
se mai disfunzioni.
Che il ritmo della mente si dislenti,
questo inspiegabilmente crea serie preoccupazioni.
Meglio si affronta il tempo quando è folto,
mezza giornata basta a sbaraccarlo.
Ma ora ai primi di luglio ogni secondo sgoccia
e l'idraulico è in ferie.

Early July

Here we are in early July and already
thought has entered the moratorium.
No dramas, no visible activity,
on the contrary, nothing but dysfunctions.
The rhythm of the mind is slowing,
which inexplicably creates serious problems.
Better to confront time when it's packed,
half a day will unpack it.
But now, in early July, the seconds are leaking
away, drop by drop,
and the plumber's on vacation.

Sono pronto ripeto, ma pronto a che?
Non alla morte cui non credo né
al brulichio d'automi che si chiama la vita.
L'altravita è un assurdo, ripeterebbe
la sua progenitrice con tutte le sue tare.
L'oltrevita è nell'etere, quell'aria da ospedale
che i felici respirano quando cadono in trappola.
L'oltrevita è nel tempo che se ne ciba
per durare più a lungo nel suo inganno.
Essere pronti non vuol dire scegliere
tra due sventure o due venture oppure
tra il tutto e il nulla. È dire io l'ho provato,
ecco il Velo, se inganna non si lacera.

I repeat, I'm ready. But ready for what?
Not for death in which I don't believe, nor
that swarming of robots called life.
Afterlife is an absurdity, it would repeat
its predecessor with all its flaws.
Life beyond is in the ether, that clinic air
breathed by the happy when they fall into the trap.
Life beyond is in time that devours itself
in order to persist in its own illusion.
Being ready doesn't mean choosing
between two mishaps or two futures or even
between all and nothing. It's saying I've tried it,
here's the Veil, if it's a fraud
nobody gets hurt.

L'imponderabile

L'incertezza è più dura del granito
e ha una sua massiccia gravitazione.
Sbrìgati dice Filli, allunga il passo
e in effetti su lei nulla gravita.
Ma l'altro è un peso piuma e il suo macigno
non può alzarlo una gru. La leggerezza
non è virtù, è destino e chi non l'ha
si può impiccare se anche col suo peso
sia più difficile.

The Imponderable

Uncertainty is harder than granite
and has its own gravitational mass.
Hurry, says our Filli, lengthen your stride
and nothing weighs you down.
But the other man's a featherweight, sandstone
even a derrick couldn't lift. Lightness
isn't virtue, it's fate,
and the man who doesn't have it
can go hang himself, though, given his weight,
that's a problem.

Lettera a Bobi

A forza di esclusioni
t'era rimasto tanto che tu potevi
stringere tra le mani; e quello era
di chi se n'accorgeva. T'ho seguito
più volte a tua insaputa. Ho percorso
più volte via Cecilia de Rittmeyer
dove avevo incontrato la tua vecchia madre,
constatato de visu il suo terrificante amore.
Del padre era rimasto il piegabaffi e forse
una bibbia evangelica. Ho assaggiato
la pleiade dei tuoi amici, oggetto
dei tuoi esperimenti più o meno falliti
di creare o distruggere felicità coniugali.
Erano i primi tuoi amici, altri
ne seguirono che non ho mai conosciuto.
S'è formata così una tua leggenda
cartacea, inattendibile. Ora dicono
ch'eri un maestro inascoltato, tu
che n'hai avuto troppi a orecchie aperte
e non ne hai diffidato. Confessore
inconfessato non potevi dare
nulla a chi già non fosse sulla tua strada.
A modo tuo hai già vinto anche se hanno perduto
tutto gli ascoltatori. Con questa lettera
che mai tu potrai leggere ti dico
addio e non aufwiedersehen e questo
in una lingua che non amavi, priva
com'è di Stimmung.

Letter to Bobi

By dint of exclusions
you could hold everything you inherited
in your two hands; and that belonged
to anyone who noticed it. On several occasions,
without your knowledge, I followed you. Several times
I walked down Via Cecilia di Rittmeyer
where I'd met your aged mother,
ascertaining *de visu* her terrifying love.
Of your father nothing but drooping mustaches
and maybe the Gospels. I savored
the *pléiade* of your friends, objects
of your more or less failed experiments
in creating or destroying conjugal bliss.
They were the friends of your youth, followed
by others whom I never met.
This was how your own implausible paper
legend was formed. They say now
that you were a master to whom no one listened—
you who had more students with open ears
than you ever suspected. Unconfessed
confessor, you could offer nothing
to those who hadn't already taken your road.
In your own way you won, though
your listeners lost everything. With this letter
which you'll never read, I bid you
adieu and not *auf Wiedersehen*, and this
in a language you didn't like, devoid
as it is of *Stimmung*.

Senza sorpresa

Senza sorpresa né odio
per le mobili turbe
di queste transumanze domenicali
in galleria, sul Corso,
sui marciapiedi già ingombri
dai tavolini dei bar
senza vizio di mente,
anzi con una clinica
imperturbabilità
io vi saluto turbe in cui vorrei
mimetizzarmi a occhi chiusi
lasciandomi guidare da quest'onda
così lenta e sicura
nella sua catastrofica insicurezza.
Ma sopravviene ora
la riflessione,
la triste acedia su cui tanto conta
il genio occulto della preservazione.
E allora si saluta
con la venerazione necessaria
il bradisismo umano,
quello che la parola non può arrestare
e si saluta senza aprire bocca,
non con gesti,
non nell'intento di scomparirvi dentro,
ma si saluta, ed è troppo, col desiderio
che tanto approdo abbia la sua proda
se anche le nostre carte non ne portino traccia.

Without Surprise

Without surprise or hatred
among the moving crowds
of these Sunday transhumances
in the arcade, on the Corso,
on sidewalks already obstructed
by cafe tables,
without defect of mind,
indeed with clinical
imperturbability,
I hail you, O you crowds, in which I'd like
to camouflage myself, eyes closed,
letting myself be guided by this wave
so slow, so secure
in its catastrophic insecurity.
But now reflection
supervenes,
that sad torpor on which the hidden
genius of preservation so much depends.
And then we hail
with the required veneration
the human bradyseism
which speech cannot arrest,
and we hail it without opening our mouths,
without gestures,
with no intention of disappearing within it,
but we hail it, too fervently, with the desire
that such a landfall should have its own harbor
though there's no trace of it on our maps.

Lettera a Malvolio

Non s'è trattato mai d'una mia fuga, Malvolio,
e neanche di un mio flair che annusi il peggio
a mille miglia. Questa è una virtù
che tu possiedi e non t'invidio anche
perché non potrei trarne vantaggio.
                                        No,
non si trattò mai d'una fuga
ma solo di un rispettabile
prendere le distanze.

Non fu molto difficile dapprima,
quando le separazioni erano nette,
l'orrore da una parte e la decenza,
oh solo una decenza infinitesima
dall'altra parte. No, non fu difficile,
bastava scantonare scolorire,
rendersi invisibili,
forse esserlo. Ma dopo.

Ma dopo che le stalle si vuotarono
l'onore e l'indecenza stretti in un solo patto
fondarono l'ossimoro permanente
e non fu più questione
di fughe e di ripari. Era l'ora
della focomelia concettuale
e il distorto era il dritto, su ogni altro
derisione e silenzio.

Letter to Malvolio

It was never a matter of my taking flight, Malvolio,
nor even some penchant of mine for sniffing out the worst
a thousand miles away. This is a virtue
you possess, and one which I don't envy you either
since there's nothing in it for me.
                                   No,
it was never a matter of taking flight,
simply a dignified
adoption of distance.

It was easy enough at the start
when the divisions were so marked—
horror on one side, and decency,
well, only an infinitesimal decency,
on the other. No, it wasn't so hard.
All it took was avoidance, fading away,
becoming invisible, maybe
being invisible. But later . . .

But later when the stables had emptied,
honor and indecency bonded in a single compact
established the permanent oxymoron
and the question was no longer one
of flight and refuge. It was the age
of the conceptual phocomele,
and the crooked was straight, and ridicule and silence
about everything else.

Fu la tua ora e non è finita.
Con quale agilità rimescolavi
materialismo storico e pauperismo evangelico,
pornografia e riscatto, nausea per l'odore
di trifola, il denaro che ti giungeva.
No, non hai torto Malvolio, la scienza del cuore
non è ancora nata, ciascuno la inventa come vuole.
Ma lascia andare le fughe ora che appena si può
cercare la speranza nel suo negativo.
Lascia che la mia fuga immobile possa dire
forza a qualcuno o a me stesso che la partita è aperta,
che la partita è chiusa per chi rifiuta
le distanze e s'affretta come tu fai, Malvolio,
perché sai che domani sarà impossibile anche
alla tua astuzia.

It was your age, and it isn't over.
With what dexterity you made your mishmash
of historical materialism and biblical pauperism,
pornography and redemption, disgust for the smell
of truffles, the money that came your way.
No, you're not wrong, Malvolio, the science of the heart
hasn't yet been born; each invents it as he likes.
But forget the flights now that one can hardly
look for hope in its own negation.
Let my motionless flight have the power to say Courage
to someone or to myself that the game is still on,
but the game is over for those who reject
distances and, like you, Malvolio, are always in a rush
since you know that tomorrow will be impossible
despite all your wiles.

p.p.c.

La mia valedizione su voi scenda
Chiliasti, amici! Amo la terra, amo

Chi me l'ha data

Chi se la riprende.

p.p.c.

Let my valediction come upon you,
Chiliasts, friends! I love the earth, I love

the One who gave it to me

the One who takes it back.

Poetic Diary:
1972

Presto o tardi

Ho creduto da bimbo che non l'uomo
si muove ma il fondale, il paesaggio.
Fu quando io, fermo, vidi srotolarsi
il lago di Lugano nel vaudeville
di un Dall'Argine che probabilmente
in omaggio a se stesso, nomen omen,
non lasciò mai la proda. Poi mi accorsi
del mio puerile inganno e ora so
che volante o pedestre, stasi o moto
in nulla differiscono. C'è chi ama
bere la vita a gocce o a garganella;
ma la bottiglia è quella, non si può
riempirla quando è vuota.

Early or Late

As a boy I thought the landscape,
the backdrop, did the moving, not man.
I know *I* wasn't moving when I saw Lake Lugano
rolling away in Dall'Argine's Lakeside Vaudeville,
though doubtless in homage to him, *nomen omen*,
it never left the shore. Later I saw through
my childish illusions, and now I know
that flying or standing, motion or stasis,
are one. Some savor life in sips,
others guzzle. But once drained,
it's the same unrefillable bottle.

Visitatori

A ogni ritorno di stagione mi dico
che anche la memoria è ciclica. Non ricordo
i miei fatti di ieri, le parole che ho detto o pubblicato
e mi assediano invece ingigantiti
volti e gesti da tempo già scacciati
dalla mente.

C'era un vecchio patrizio nel Tirolo alto
che a guerra appena finite accolse nella sua reggia
con tovaglie di Fiandra, porcellane di Sèvres,
vini della Mosella, delikatessen
lo sbracato invasore ch'ero io, offuscato
dalla vergogna, quasi incerto se
prosternarmi ai suoi piedi.

Più tardi ancora il grande Däubler poeta
della luce del Nord, un nibelungo barbuto
di immense mole che sfonda la poltrona
e sillaba i miei poveri versi di sconosciuto
miscelando due lingue, la sua e la mia perfette
come mai ho ascoltato. È una memoria o un sogno?

Se mi apparisse Omero o almeno il più buio Callimaco
o altro ancora più piccolo ma scritto nella storia
mi sarebbe più facile di sconfiggere il sogno
e dirgli retrocedi, mi sveglierò e sarò libero
dall'incubo. Ma no, questi che parlano
la stessa lingua hanno lasciato tracce
nell'anagrafe o altrove.

Visitors

With each returning season I remind myself
that memory is cyclical too. I don't remember
what I did yesterday, the words I spoke or published;
instead I'm assailed by faces and gestures
long since driven from mind, and now grown
gigantic.

There was an old patrician in the upper Tyrol
who shortly after the war invited me
to his palatial residence—Flemish table-cloths,
Sèvres china, Mosel wines, and *delicatessen*—
unbuttoned invader that I was, a cloud of confusion
and shame, almost wondering whether to prostrate myself
at his feet.

Again, later still, it was the great Däubler, poet
of the Northern Lights, a bearded Nibelung
of immense bulk who plumped down in the armchair
and declaimed my poor tyro verses, syllable by syllable,
jumbling two languages, his and mine, as perfectly
as I ever heard. Memory or dream?

If Homer appeared, or at least the obscurer Callimachus,
or some other poet, more minor but still historical,
it would be easier to defeat the dream and tell it
to go back whence it came. I'd wake, free
of my nightmare. But no, people who speak
the same language have left traces of themselves
in birth-registries or elsewhere.

Una volta un vegliardo mi raccontò
di aver dormito lunghi anni accanto
a un cestino di fichi nella speranza
di ritrovarli freschi al suo risveglio.
Ma il sonno non durò anni sessantasei
e il record dell'Oasiano della leggenda
non fu certo battuto. Nel cestino
più nulla di appetibile, formiche.
Ritenterò mi disse di sospendere il tempo.
Escomparve nel sogno. (Se fu sogno
o realtà me lo sto chiedendo ancora).

Once an old man told me
how he'd fallen asleep for many years
next to a basket of figs, hoping
to find them still fresh when he woke.
But his sleep didn't last sixty-six years
and the record of the legendary Oasian
remained unbroken. The basket held
nothing edible, only ants.
I'll have one more try at suspending time, he said,
and vanished into his dream. (Whether it was dream
or reality still stumps me.)

L'odore dell'eresia

Fu miss Petrus, l'agiografa e segretaria
di Tyrrell, la sua amante? Sì, fu la risposta
del barnabita e un brivido d'orrore
serpeggiò tra parenti, amici e altri
ospiti occasionali.

Io appena un bambino, indifferente
alla questione, il barnabita era anche
un discreto tapeur di pianoforte,
e a quattro mani, forse a quattro piedi
avevamo cantato e pesticciato
'In questa tomba oscura' e altrettali
amenità.

Che fosse in odore di eresia
pareva ignoto al parentado. Quando
fu morto e già dimenticato appresi
ch'era sospeso a divinis e restai a bocca aperta.
Sospeso sì, ma da chi? Da che cosa e perché?
A mezz'aria attaccato a un filo?
E il divino sarebbe un gancio a cui ci si appende?
Si può annusarlo come qualsiasi odore?

Solo più tardi appresi il significato
della parola e non restai affatto
col respire sospeso. Il vecchio prete
mi pare di rivederlo nella pineta

The Odor of Heresy

Was Miss Petre, Tyrell's hagiographer
and secretary, his mistress too? Yes,
the Barnabite answered, and a shudder of horror
slithered over relatives, friends, and other
occasional guests.

Little more than a child, I had no interest
in the question. Besides, the Barnabite
was passably good at playing the piano,
and with our four hands, and maybe our four feet,
we'd sung and pounded out
In questa tomba oscura and other such
amenities.

That he smelled of heresy
was, it seems, unknown to his relatives.
When he was dead and already forgotten, I learned
he'd been suspended *a divinis*, which shocked me.
Suspended, sure, but by whom? From what, and why?
Was he dangling from a wire in mid-air?
And was the "divine" a sort of hook for hanging things?
Could you sniff heresy like other smells?

Only later did I learn the meaning
of the word, and it didn't send me into shock.
Not a bit. In imagination I see the old priest once more,
there in the pine-grove long since burnt down, bent

ch'è bruciata da un pezzo, un po' curvo su testi
miasmatici, un balsamo per lui. E l'odore
che si diffonde non ha nulla a che fare
col divino o il demonico, soffi di voce, pneumi
di cui è traccia solo in qualche carta illeggibile.

over noxious texts which to him were balsam.
And the smell he gives off has nothing to do
with divine or demonic voices, breathings,
neumes of which, but for a few illegible sheets,
not a note remains.

Le acque alte

Mi sono inginocchiato con delirante amore
sulla fonte Castalia
ma non filo d'acqua rifletteva
la mia immagine.
Non ho veduto mai
le acque dei piranha. Chi vi s'immerge
torna alla riva scheletro scarnificato.

Eppure
altre acque lavorano con noi,
per noi, su noi con un'indifferente
e mostruosa opera di recupero.
Le acque si riprendono
ciò che hanno dato: le asseconda il loro
invisibile doppio, il tempo; e un flaccido
gonfio risciacquamento ci deruba
da quando lasciammo le pinne per mettere fuori gli arti,
una malformazione, una beffa che ci ha lasciato gravidi
di cattiva coscienza e responsabilità.

Parve che la ribollente zavorra su cui mi affaccio,
rottami, casse, macchine ammassate
giù nel cortile,
la fumosa colata che se ne va
per conto suo e ignora la nostra esistenza,
parve che tutto questo fosse la prova del nove
che siamo qui per qualcosa un trabocchetto o uno scopo.
Parve, non pare ... In altri tempi scoppiavano

Flood Tides

Frantic with love, I knelt
at the Castalian Spring
but no freshet reflected
my image.

I have never seen
the piranha's native waters where swimmers
wash back ashore, bones picked clean.

And yet
other waters work with us,
for us, and on us, with an indifferent
monstrous effort of recuperation.
What once they gave,
the waters take back, aided by Time, their unseen
double. And the laving of this feeble, tumid tide
has preyed on us since we abandoned fins
to sprout these limbs of ours—a malformation,
a sad joke which saddled us
with responsibility and bad conscience.

The seething junk my window overlooks—
trash, crates, cars heaped
in the courtyard below,
the slow, smoky flow that streams away
on its own account, ignoring our existence—
all this seemed final proof
that we're here for something, a trap, a goal.
Seemed, not *seems* . . . Once upon a time

castagne sulla brace, brillava qualche lucignolo
sui doni natalizi. Ora non piace più
al demone delle acque darci atto che noi
suoi spettatori e còrrei siamo pur sempre noi.

chestnuts burst in the hot coals, tapers glowed
on the Christmas presents. Now the demon
of the waters no longer bothers apprising us
that we, his spectators and accomplices,
are still only ourselves.

Per una nona strofa

Per finire sul 9 mi abbisognava
un piròpo galante, poche sillabe.
Ma non ho il taglio e la misura dei
decadenti augustei. Troppo è più dura
la materia del dire e del sentire.
Non si parla più d'anni ma di millenni
e quando s'entra in questi non è in gioco
il vivo o il morto la ragione o il torto.

For a Ninth Stanza

To finish on the 9th I needed
a little gallantry, short and sweet.
But I lack the clipped precision
of the classicizing Augustans. The stuff
of speech and feeling is too much, and tougher.
People no longer talk of years but millennia
and when that's the case, living or dead,
right or wrong, just don't matter.

La Fama e il Fisco

Mi hanno telefonato per chiedermi che penso
di Didone e altre dive oggi resurte
alla tv;
ma i classici restano in alto, appena raggiungibili
con la scala.
Più tardi lo scaffale ha toccato il cielo,
le nubi ed è scomparso dalla memoria.
Nulla resta di classico fuori delle bottiglie
brandite come stocchi da un ciarlatano del video.
Nulla resta di vero se non le impronte
digitali lasciate da un *monssù Travet*
su un foglio spiegazzato malchiuso da uno spillo.
Là dentro non c'è Didone o altre immortali.
Non c'è mestizia né gioia, solo una cifra e un pizzico
di immondizia.

Fame and the Fisc

They phoned to ask me what I think
of Dido and other divas being resurrected
nowadays on T.V.;
but the classics are way above us, unreachable
except with a ladder.
Later, the bookcase touched the sky,
the clouds, and vanished from memory.
Nothing's left of the classic but bottles
brandished like daggers by a video huckster.
Nothing's left of truth but the fingerprints
left by a certain *Monssù Travet*
on a piece of badly crumpled paper loosely pinned.
There's no Dido in it or other immortal ladies.
No joy, no grief, only a number with a scumbling
of dung.

Chi tiene i fili

Chi tiene i fili ne sa più di noi.
Chi non li tiene ne sa di più e di meno.
Un incontro tra l'uno e l'altro; ed ecco
il disastro che avviene, la catastrofe
senza né più né meno.

He who pulls the strings . . .

He who pulls the strings knows more of them than we.
He who doesn't pull them knows both more and less.
The two meet; and pow!
disaster, pure catastrophe—
"no more" and "no less."

Jaufré

a Goffredo Parise

Jaufré passa le notti incapsulato
in una botte. Alla primalba s'alza
un fischione e lo sbaglia. Poco dopo
c'è troppa luce e lui si riaddormenta.
È l'inutile impresa di chi tenta
di rinchiudere il tutto in qualche niente
che si rivela solo perché si sente.

Jaufré

for Goffredo Parise

Jaufré spends the nights
cooped in a blind. At daybreak
a widgeon whistles up, and he misses.
Minutes later there's too much light
and he falls back asleep.
A hopeless task—this effort to cram
everything into this bit of nothingness
that reveals itself only when audible.

Il cavallo

Io non son il cavallo
di Caracalla come Benvolio crede;
non corro il derby, non mi cibo di erbe,
non fui uomo di corsa ma neppure
di trotto. Tentai di essere
un uomo e già era troppo
per me (e per lui).

The Horse

I'm not Caracalla's horse,
as Benvolio believes; I don't run
in the derby, I don't like grass.
As a man, I was no racer, I wasn't even
a pacer. I tried to be
a man and that was more than enough
for me (and him).

Notturno

Sarà che la civetta di Minerva
sta per aprire le ali. Ma non è sosta
nel rifornimento
dello spaccio di cui noi siamo appena
rimasugli svenduti per liquidazione.
Eppure l'avevamo creato con orgoglio
a nostra somiglianza il robottone
della fluente e ghiotta infinità.
O cieli azzurri o nobili commerci
non solo coi Celesti! Ora anche la Dea
nostra serva e padrona chiude gli occhi
per non vederci.

Nocturne

Maybe Minerva's owl is ready
to spread her wings. But there's no let-up
in resupplying that sale
in which we're merely remnants
dumped for clearance.
Still, we were proud of creating
him in our image—that giant robot
of fluent, glutton infinity.
O blue skies O noble commerce
and not only with Celestials! Now even the Goddess,
our servant and mistress, shuts her eyes
so as not to see us.

Le Figure

Estasiato dalla sua ipallage
il poeta trasse un respiro
di sollievo ma c'era un buco nel poema
che si allargò, fu voragine
e lo scagliò nella cantina dove
si mettono le trappole per i tropi.
Di lui nulla restò. Solo qualche Figura,
scruta obsoleta, disse meglio così.

Figures of Speech

In ecstasy with his hypallage
the poet heaved a sigh
of relief, but his poem had a hole in it,
which widened, became a chasm,
and flung him into that basement where
traps for tropes are set.
Nothing was left of him. Only two or three
Figures of Speech, *scruta obsoleta*, said
it's better this way.

Il terrore di esistere

Le famiglie dei grandi buffi
dell'operetta si sono estinte
e con esse anche il genere comico, sostituito
dal tribale tan tan degli assemblaggi.

È una grande sventura nascere piccoli
e la peggiore quella di chi rimbambisce
mimando la stoltizia che paventa
una qualche improbabile identità.

Il terrore di esistere non è cosa
da prender sottogamba, anzi i matusa
ne hanno stivato tanta nei loro sottoscala
che a stento e con vergogna potevano nascondervisi.

E la vergogna non è, garzon bennato, che un primo
barlume della vita. Se muore prima di nascere
nulla se le accompagna che possa dire noi
siamo noi ed è un fatto appena credibile.

Nell'anno settantacinquesimo e più della mia vita
sono disceso nei miei ipogei e il deposito
era là intatto. Vorrei spargerlo a piene mani
in questi sanguinosi giorni di carnevale.

The Terror of Existence

The families of the great buffoons
of operetta have become extinct,
and with them the comic genre, replaced
by the tribal tomtoms of technology.

Being born small is a great misfortune,
but the worst is becoming a child again,
aping the silliness that flinches
from some unlikely identity.

The terror of existence is not to be taken
lightly; in fact, our Methusalehs have stashed
away so much that their storerooms can hardly
hide them and their shame.

And shame, old boy, is only a first
glimmering of life. If it dies before it's born,
nothing afterwards can equal its power of telling us
the almost unbelievable fact—that we're we.

In the seventy-fifth year plus of my life
I went down to my basement and found my store
of shame intact. I'd like to squander it,
all of it, in these bloody days of Carnival.

Verboten

Dicono che nella grammatica di Kafka
manca il futuro. Questa la scoperta
di chi serbò l'incognito e con buone ragioni.
Certo costui teme le conseguenze
flagranti o addirittura conflagranti
del suo colpo di genio. E Kafka stesso,
la sinistra cornacchia, andrebbe al rogo
nell'effigie e nelle opere, d'altronde
largamente invendute.

Verboten

They say the future tense is missing
in Kafka's grammar—the discovery of someone
who remained anonymous, and with good reason.
Clearly he dreads the consequences,
the flagrant or flat-out conflagrations
of his own stroke of genius. And Kafka himself,
that croaking raven, would be burnt at the stake
in effigy or in his works, which in any case
don't sell.

Quel che più conta

A forza d'inzeppare
in una qualche valigia di finto cuoio
gonfia a scoppiare
tutti i lacerti della nostra vita
ci siamo detti che il politeismo
non era da buttar via.

Le abbiamo più volte incontrate,
viste di faccia o di sbieco
le nostre mezze divinità e fu stolto
chiederne una maggiore,
quasi una mongolfiera
totale dello spirito, una bolla
di spazio soffiata di cui noi fossimo gli ospiti
e i sudditi adoranti.

E salutiamo con umiltà gli iddii
che ci hanno dato una mano durante il nostro viaggio,
veneriamo i loro occhi, i loro piedi
se mai n'ebbero, i doni
che ci offersero, i loro insulti e scherni,
prosterniamoci alle loro ombre se pure
ne furono e andiamo incontro al tempo,
all'avvenire che non è più vero
del passato perché tutto che riempie un vuoto
non fu né mai sarà più pieno dei
custodi dell'Eterno, gli invisibili.

What Matters Most

By dint of stuffing
a few leatherette suitcases
full to splitting
with all the sinews of our life
we were told that polytheism
wasn't to be trashed.

We met them on several occasions,
face to face or brushing by,
our demigods, and it was stupid
to ask for an even bigger,
nearly absolute, hot-air balloon
of the spirit, a blown bubble
of space of which we were
adoring subjects and guests.

And we humbly greet the gods
who lent us a helping hand on our journey,
we worship their eyes, their feet
(if they had any), the gifts
they gave us, their jeers and insults,
let's prostrate ourselves in their shadows
(if they cast any) and go and face time,
that future which is no more true than the past
since whatever fills a void completely
never was, and never will be full of the invisible ones,
the guardians of the Eternal.

Kingfisher

Praticammo con cura il carpe diem,
tentammo di acciuffare chi avesse pelo o escrescenze,
gettammo l'amo senza che vi abboccasse
tinca o barbo (e di trote non si parli).
Ora siamo al rovescio e qui restiamo attenti
se sia mai una lenza che ci agganci.
Ma il Pescatore nicchia perché la nostra polpa
anche al cartoccio o in carpione non trova più clienti.

Kingfisher

We scrupulously practiced *carpe diem*,
we tried to catch anything with excrescences or skin,
we cast our flies, though the hook was never taken
by tench or barbel (no chance of trout!).
Now the situation's reversed; we're the ones
anxiously waiting to be hooked.
But the Fisherman takes his time:
even *en papillote* or marinaded,
our flesh is not in demand.

La pendola a carillon

La vecchia pendola a carillon
veniva dalla Francia forse dal tempo
del secondo Impero.
Non dava trilli o rintocchi ma esalava
più che suonare tanto n'era fioca la voce
l'entrata di Escamillo o le campane
di Corneville: le novità di quando
qualcuno l'acquistò: forse il proavo
finito al manicomio e sotterrato
senza rimpianti, necrologi o altre
notizie che turbassero i suoi non nati nepoti.
I quali vennero poi e vissero senza memoria
di chi portò quell'oggetto tra inospiti mura sferzate
da furibonde libecciate—e chi
di essi ne udì il richiamo? Era una sveglia
beninteso che mai destò nessuno
che non fosse già sveglio. Io solo un'alba
regolarmente insonne traudii l'ectoplasma
vocale, il soffio della toriada,
ma appena per un attimo. Poi la voce
della boîte non si estinse ma si fece parola
poco udibile e disse non c'è molla né carica
che un giorno non si scarichi. Io ch'ero
il Tempo lo abbandono. Ed a te che sei l'unico
mio ascoltatore dico cerca di vivere
nel fuordeltempo, quello che nessuno
può misurare. Poi la voce tacque
e l'orologio per molti anni ancora
rimase appeso al muro. Probabilmente
v'è ancora la sua traccia sull'intonaco.

The Chiming Pendulum Clock

The old pendulum clock
probably came from France in the days
of the Second Empire.
It chimed so faintly it neither tinkled nor pealed,
but rather exhaled Escamillo's entering motif
in *Les Cloches de Corneville*—novelties
when the clock was bought, perhaps
by the great-grandfather who ended his days
in an asylum and was buried with no mourning,
obituaries, or any notices which might have embarrassed
grandchildren still unborn.
They came later, living their lives with no memory
of the man who lugged that object within unwelcoming
walls lashed by raging southwesters—and did anyone of them
ever hear it chime? It had a well-meaning call,
arousing nobody who wasn't already awake.
Only I, plagued by early morning insomnia, made out
that weak vocal ectoplasm, the blowing of the *toriada*,
but only for an instant. Then the voice
from the *boîte* faded away, not completely, but became
a barely audible whisper, saying: No spring,
no mechanism exists that won't someday wear out.
I, who once was Time, renounce time. And to you,
my one and only listener, I say: Try living
in the timeless moment, which can't be clocked.
Then the voice stopped,
and for many years the clock stayed where it was,
hanging on the wall. No doubt its outline
is still there, in the plaster.

C'è chi muore . . .

C'è chi muore per noi. È cosa di tutti i giorni
e accade anche a me stesso per qualcuno.
Che sacrifizio orrendo questa compensazione
che dovrebbe salvarci tutti en bloc,
bravi turisti che spendono poco e non vedono nulla.

Così d'accordo camminano teologia economia
semiologia cibernetica e altro ancora ignoto
che sta incubando, di cui noi saremo
nutrimento e veleno, pieno e vuoto.

Others die for us . . .

Others die for us. It's an everyday event
which happens to me too, on behalf of others.
What a frightful sacrifice, this recompensation
which ought to save us all *en masse*,
good tourists who spend little and see nothing!

So they proceed, hand-in-hand—theology,
economics, semiotics, cybernetics and other
disciplines still unknown now incubating,
of which we'll be pap and poison, fullness and void.

A un grande filosofo

in devoto ricordo

Una virtù dei Grandi è di essere sordi
a tutto il molto o il poco che non li riguardi.
Trascurando i famelici e gli oppressi
alquanto alieni dai vostri interessi
divideste lo Spirito in quattro spicchi
che altri rimpastò in uno: donde ripicchi, faide
nel gregge degli yesmen professionali.
Vivete in pace nell'eterno: foste
giusto senza saperlo, senza volerlo.
Lo spirito non è nei libri, l'avete saputo,
e nemmeno si trova nella vita e non certo
nell'altra vita. La sua natura resta
in disparte. Conosce il nostro vivere
(lo sente), anzi vorrebbe farne parte
ma niente gli è possibile per l'ovvia
contradizion che nol consente.

To a Great Philosopher

in affectionate remembrance
One virtue of the Great is being deaf
to anything, large or small, that doesn't concern them.
By ignoring the starving and oppressed
so alien to your interests,
you divided the Spirit into four chunks
which others worked back into one: whence feuds
and repercussions in the pack of professional
yes-men. You great ones live at peace
in the eternal: without knowing it, without
even wanting it, you were right. You knew the spirit
can't be found in books, is not even found even in life,
far less in another life. Its nature
is apartness. It acknowledges our existence
(feels it), would even like to participate,
but can't, thanks to the clearly
unconsenting contradiction.

Il paguro

Il paguro non guarda per il sottile
se s'infila in un guscio che non è il suo.
Ma resta un eremita. Il mio male è
che se mi sfilo dal mio non posso entrare nel tuo.

The Hermit Crab

The hermit crab doesn't look too closely,
he just crawls into a shell that isn't his.
But remains a hermit. That's my hang-up:
if I leave my shell, I can't crawl into yours.

In un giardino 'italiano'

La vecchia tartaruga cammina male, beccheggia
perché le fu troncata una zampetta anteriore.
Quando un verde mantello entra in agitazione
è lei che arranca invisibile in geometrie di trifogli
e torna al suo rifugio.
Da quanti anni? Qui restano incerti
giardiniere e padrone.
Mezzo secolo o più. O si dovrà risalire
al generale Pelloux . . .
Non c'è un'età per lei: tutti gli strappi
sono contemporanei.

In an "Italian" Garden

Since one of his hind legs was cut off,
the old turtle walks with a lurch.
When a lush green lawn starts to quiver,
it's the turtle limping invisibly through clover
geometries back to his shelter.
How long has he been lame? On this point
gardener and owner are both uncertain.
Fifty years or more. Or earlier still,
back in the days of General Pelloux . . .
To the tortoise all ages are one, all lesions
contemporary.

Sulla spiaggia

Ora il chiarore si fa più diffuso.
Ancora chiusi gli ultimi ombrelloni.
Poi appare qualcuno che trascina
il suo gommone.
La venditrice d'erbe viene e affonda
sulla rena la sua mole, un groviglio
di vene varicose. È un monolito
diroccato dai picchi di Lunigiana.
Quando mi parla resto senza fiato,
le sue parole sono la Verità.
Ma tra poco sarà qui il cafarnao
delle carni, dei gesti e delle barbe.
Tutti i lemuri umani avranno al collo
croci e catene. Quanta religione.
E c'è chi s'era illuso di ripetere
l'exploit di Crusoe!

On the Beach

Now the light grows and widens.
The farthest beach-umbrellas are still closed.
Then somebody shows, dragging
a rubber mattress.
The market-woman arrives and plumps
her bulk onto the sand, a maze
of varicose veins. She's a monolith, solid
marble toppled from the peaks of Lunigiana.
When she speaks to me, I'm breathless,
her words are Truth.
But soon there'll be a holy mess
of flesh, beards, gestures.
All the human lemurs will be sporting crosses
and chains. The legions of religion!
And some poor joker dreamed of repeating
the feat of Robinson Crusoe!

I nuovi iconografi

Si sta allestendo l'iconografia
di massimi scrittori e presto anche
dei minimi. Vedremo dove hanno abitato,
se in regge o in bidonvilles, le loro scuole
e latrine se interne o appiccicate
all'esterno con tubi penzolanti
su stabbi di maiali, studieremo gli oroscopi
di ascendenti, propaggini e discendenti,
le strade frequentate, i lupanari se mai
ne sopravviva alcuno all'onorata Merlin,
toccheremo i loro abiti, gli accappatoi, i clisteri
se usati e quando e quanti, i menù degli alberghi,
i pagherò firmati, le lozioni
o pozioni o decotti, la durata
dei loro amori, eterei o carnivori
o solo epistolari, leggeremo
cartelle cliniche, analisi e se cercassero il sonno
nel Baffo o nella Bibbia. Così la storia
trascura gli epistemi per le emorroidi
mentre vessilli olimpici sventolano sui pennoni
e sventole di mitraglia forniscono i contorni.

The New Iconographers

They're assembling the iconography
of the greatest writers and, before long,
the least. We'll soon have a peek
at where they lived, in palaces or *bidonvilles*,
the schools they attended, their privies,
whether inside or out, with pipes protruding
over pigsties; we'll pore over the horoscopes
of their ancestors, children, and descendants,
the streets where they lived, and their brothels
(if any survived Senator Merlin's legislation);
we'll finger their clothes, bathrobes, enema bags
(if they used enemas, and when, and where), their hotel
menus, I.O.U.'s, their lotions
or potions, or decoctions, the length
of their love affairs, ethereal or carnivorous,
or merely epistolary; we'll peruse
their medical records, urinalyses, and whether
they dozed off reading Baffo or the Bible.
                    So history neglects
the sciences in the name of hemorrhoids
while Olympic ensigns flutter on the pennants
and the sputter of fanning machine-guns
garnishes the proceedings.

Asor

Asor, nome gentile (il suo retrogrado
è il più bel fiore),
non ama il privatismo in poesia.
Ne ha ben donde o ne avrebbe se la storia
producesse un quid simile o un'affine
sostanza, il che purtroppo non accade.
La poesia non è fatta per nessuno,
non per altri e nemmeno per chi la scrive.
Perché nasce? Non nasce affatto e dunque
non è mai nata. *Sta* come una pietra
o un granello di sabbia. Finirà
con tutto il resto. Se sia tardi o presto
lo dirà l'escatologo, il funesto
mistagogo che è nato a un solo parto
col tempo—e lo detesta.

Asor

Asor, a gracious name (spelled backwards,
the loveliest of flowers),
dislikes privatism in poetry.
With good reason for it, or he would have, if history
produced any such thing or some related
substance, which, alas, it doesn't.
Poetry is not produced for anyone,
not for others, not even for the poet.
Why is it born? It isn't born at all,
so it never was born. It *is*, like a stone
or a grain of sand. It will end up
like everything else. Whether sooner or later
we'll learn from the eschatologist, the gloomiest
mystagogue ever born in a single birth
with time—which he despises.

Ancora ad Annecy

a G.F.

Quando introdussi un franco
nella fessura di una slot machine
raccolsi nelle mani un diluvio d'argento
perché la mangiasoldi s'era guastata.
Mi sentii incolpevole e il tesoro
fu tosto dilapidate da Cirillo e da me.
Allora non pensai al nobiliare ostello
che t'ha ospitata prima che la casa
dei doganieri fosse sorta, quasi
come una rupe nel ricordo. Era una
storia più tua che mia e non l'ho mai saputa.
Bastò una manciatella di monete
a creare l'orribile afasia?
O si era forse un po' brilli? Non ho voluto mai chiederlo
a Cirillo.

At Annécy Again

for G.F.

I inserted a franc
in a slot-machine,
and because the one-armed bandit was broken,
I scooped up a river of silver.
I felt no guilt and the treasure
was quickly squandered by Cirillo and me.
I wasn't thinking then of the aristocratic house
that sheltered you before the coastguard
station—cliff-like in my memory—
was built. It was more your story
than mine, and I never grasped it.
Was that little handful of coins enough
to provoke that dreadful aphasia?
Or was I a little crocked? I've never wanted to ask
Cirillo.

Il principe della Festa

Ignoro dove sia il principe della Festa,
Quegli che regge il mondo e le altre sfere.
Ignoro se sia festa o macelleria
quello che scorgo se mi affaccio alla finestra.
Se è vero che la pulce vive in sue dimensioni
(così ogni altro animale) che non sono le nostre,
se è vero che il cavallo vede l'uomo più grande
quasi due volte, allora non c'è occhio umano che basti.
Forse un eterno buio si stancò, sprizzò fuori
qualche scintilla. O un'eterea luce
si maculò trovando se stessa insopportabile.
Oppure il principe ignora le sue fatture
o può vantarsene solo in dosi omeopatiche.
Ma è sicuro che un giorno sul suo seggio
peseranno altre natiche. È già l'ora.

The Lord of the Revels

I don't know where he is, the Lord of the Revels,
Ruler of the world and the other spheres.
I don't know if what I see from my window
is feast or butchery. If it's true that the flea
(like every other animal) actually lives
in his own dimensions, and if those aren't ours;
if to the horse's eye men look twice as large
as they really are, then human eyes are inadequate.
Maybe eternal darkness got weary and showered out
a couple of sparks. Or an ethereal light,
bored with purity, spotted itself.
Or else the Lord is ignorant of his own creations
or can boast of them only in homeopathic doses.
But one thing's certain: someday other buttocks
will oppress his throne. The time is ripe.

Non c'è morte

Fu detto che non si può vivere senza la carapace
di una mitologia.
Non sarebbe gran male se non fosse che sempre
l'ultima è la peggiore.

I vecchi numi erano confortevoli,
non importa se ostili.
I nuovi ci propinano una vile
benevolenza ma ignorano la nostra sorte.

Non solo sono al buio di chi vive
ma restano all'oscuro di se stessi.
Pure hanno un volto amico anche se uccidono
e non è morte dove mai fu nascita.

There's No Dying

It's been said that life is impossible without the carapace
of a mythology.
Which would be tolerable except that the last mythology
is always the worst.

The old divinities were comfortable,
though occasionally unfriendly.
The new gods dispense a base benevolence
but know nothing of our fate.

Not only are they in the dark about the living,
they're even benighted about themselves.
Still, they look friendly, even when they kill,
and there's no dying where there wasn't a birth.

Gli uomini si sono organizzati
come se fossero mortali;
senza di che non si avrebbero
giorni, giornali, cimiteri, scampoli
di ciò che non è più.

Gli uomini si sono organizzati
come se fossero immortali;
senza di che sarebbe stolto credere
che nell'essente viva ciò che fu.

Men have organized themselves
as though they were mortal;
otherwise there'd be no day,
no dailies, cemeteries, and relics
of what no longer exists.

Men have organized themselves
as though they were immortal;
if not, it would be stupid to believe
that what *was* is alive in what *is*.

Non era tanto facile abitare
nel cavallo di Troia.
Vi si era così stretti da sembrare
acciughe in salamoia.
Poi gli altri sono usciti, io restai dentro,
incerto sulle regole del combattimento.

Ma questo lo so ora, non allora,
quando ho tenuto in serbo per l'ultimo atto,
e decisivo, il meglio delle mie forze.
Fu un atto sterminato, quasi l'auto
sacramental dei vili nella scorza
di un quadrupede che non fu mai fatto.

Life in the Trojan Horse
was no picnic.
We were packed in
like anchovies in a can.
When the others left,
I stayed inside, unsure
of the rules of war.

Now I know what I didn't then,
when I hoarded my noblest powers
for the final, the decisive act.
Which was an act that had no end,
almost the *auto sacramental*,
of the baseborn in the hide
of an unrealized quadruped.

Annetta

Perdona Annetta se dove tu sei
(non certo tra di noi, i sedicenti
vivi) poco ti giunge il mio ricordo.
Le tue apparizioni furono per molti anni
rare e impreviste, non certo da te volute.
Anche i luoghi (la rupe dei doganieri,
la foce del Bisagno dove ti trasformasti in Dafne)
non avevano senso senza di te.
Di certo resta il gioco delle sciarade incatenate
o incastrate che fossero di cui eri maestra.
Erano veri spettacoli in miniatura.
Vi recitai la parte di Leonardo
(Bistolfi ahimè, non l'altro), mi truccai da leone
per ottenere il 'primo' e quanto al nardo
mi aspersi di profumi. Ma non bastò la barba
che mi aggiunsi prolissa e alquanto sudicia.
Occorreva di più, una statua viva
da me scolpita. E fosti tu a balzare
su un plinto traballante di dizionari
miracolosa palpitante ed io
a modellarti con non so quale aggeggio.
Fu il mio solo successo di teatrante
domestico. Ma so che tutti gli occhi
posavano su te. Tuo era il prodigio.

Altra volta salimmo fino alla torre
dove sovente un passero solitario
modulava il motivo che Massenet
imprestò al suo Des Grieux.

Annetta

Forgive me, Annetta, if my memory
just barely reaches you where you are now
(not, to be sure, amongst us, the so-called
living). For many years your apparitions were few
and unexpected, clearly not what you willed.
Even the places (the cliff of the coastguard station,
the mouth of the Bisagno where you changed
into Daphne) had no meaning in your absence.
Of course I remember the charades,
linked or complex, of which you were mistress—
genuine miniature star-performances.
I played the role of Leonardo (Bistolfi,
alas, not da Vinci). I dressed up as a lion
to win the first prize and sprayed myself with perfume
in place of spikenard. But the beard
I added—full-length and rather sweaty—
wouldn't do. I needed something more, a living statue
sculpted by me. And it was you who leapt up
on a wobbly pedestal of dictionaries, miraculously
a-quiver, while I modelled you
with god knows what gadget. It was my only success
as a family actor. But I know that all eyes
were riveted on you. The miracle was you.

Another day we climbed the tower
where a solitary thrush was singing variations
on Des Grieux's theme in Massenet.

Più tardi ne uccisi uno fermo sull'asta
della bandiera: il solo mio delitto
che non so perdonarmi. Ma ero pazzo
e non di te, pazzo di gioventù,
pazzo della stagione più ridicola
della vita. Ora sto
a chiedermi che posto tu hai avuto
in quella mia stagione. Certo un senso
allora inesprimibile, più tardi
non l'oblio ma una punta che feriva
quasi a sangue. Ma allora eri già morta
e non ho mai saputo dove e come.
Oggi penso che tu sei stata un genio
di pura inesistenza, un'agnizione
reale perché assurda. Lo stupore
quando s'incarna è lampo che ti abbaglia
e si spenge. Durare potrebbe essere
l'effetto di una droga nel creato,
in un medium di cui non si ebbe mai
alcuna prova.

Later, I killed a thrush perching on the flagpole—
the one crime I've never forgiven myself.
But I was crazy-wild—not over you, crazy with youth,
wild with life's most ludicrous season.
Now I have to ask myself:
what was your place in that season of mine?
Clearly a feeling for which I had no words
at the time; and later, not forgetfulness,
but a wound so painful I almost bled.
But by then you had already died,
and I never knew how or why.
Today I think of you as a genius
of pure non-existence, a recognition
made real by its absurdity.
Amazement, when it takes on flesh,
is a flash of lightning, which blinds and then blacks out.
Endurance might be the effect of some drug
on the created, in a medium of which there was never
the slightest proof.

La caccia

Si dice che il poeta debba andare
a caccia dei suoi contenuti.
E si afferma altresì che le sue prede
debbono corrispondere a ciò che avviene nel mondo,
anzi a quel che sarebbe un mondo che fosse migliore.

Ma nel mondo peggiore si può impallinare
qualche altro cacciatore oppure un pollo
di batteria fuggito dalla gabbia.
Quanto al migliore non ci sarà bisogno
di poeti. Ruspanti saremo tutti.

The Hunt

Poets, they say, should go hunting
in quest of their content.
They also assert that the poets' quarry
must relate to events in the world,
or better yet, to making that world better.

But in the worse world you can pump birdshot
into other hunters or maybe a brooder
chick who's flown the coop.
As for the better world, there'll be no room there
for poets. We'll all be out scratching

Tra chiaro e oscuro

Tra chiaro e oscuro c'è un velo sottile.
Tra buio e notte il velo si assottiglia.
Tra notte e nulla il velo è quasi impalpabile.
La nostra mente fa corporeo anche il nulla.
Ma è allora
che cominciano i grandi rovesciamenti,
la furiosa passione per il tangibile,
non quello elefantiaco, mostruoso
che nessuna mano può chiudere in sé,
ma la minugia, il fuscello che neppure
il più ostinato bricoleur può scorgere.
Il Leviatano uccide, non può crescere oltre
e scoppia,
ma quello che ci resta sotto le unghie
anche se usciamo appena dalla manicure,
quello è ancora la prova che siamo polvere
e torneremo polvere e tutto questo
è polvere di vita, il meglio e il tutto.

Between Light and Dark

Between light and dark there is a thin veil.
Between dark and night the veil attenuates.
Between night and nothing the veil is almost impalpable.
Our minds confer body even on nothingness.
But then
the great reversals begin,
the rage for the tangible—
not the elephantine, monstrous reversal
which no hand can possibly contain,
but little things, the catgut string, the twig that even
the most dogged *bricoleur* can't detect.
Leviathan kills, it can't get larger,
it explodes,
but what lies under our fingernails—
even though we're fresh from the manicurist—
is one more proof that we are dust,
that we'll return to dust, and that all this
is the dust of life—the best of it,
all.

Opinioni

Non si è mai saputo se la vita
sia ciò che si vive o ciò che si muore.
Ma poi sarebbe inutile saperlo
ammesso che sia utile l'impossibile.

Se dire che la vita è una sostanza,
una materia è mera cantafavola,
anche più stolto è crederla una fumata
che condensa, o rimuove, ogni altro fumo.

Ma no, dice Calpurnio, è appena un suono
mai pronunziato perché non è nell'aria
nostra, ma nella sua. È non c'è nome
neppure scritto dove l'aria manca.

Opinions

Whether what we live or die
is life, there's no way of ever knowing.
But even if what can't be done were useful,
the knowing would be useless anyway.

If the view that life is a substance,
a physical thing, is merely a long-winded myth,
the notion of life as a smoke that condenses,
or dissolves, all other smoke, is more fatuous still.

But no, says Calpurnius. Life is hardly a sound,
never uttered since it exists in its own air,
not in ours. And where there's no air,
a thing has no name and can't even be written.

Un millenarista

Non s'incrementa (sic) la produzione
se si protegge l'Alma Mater (Alma?).
Tertium non datur; ma ci sarà un terzo,
il solo uomo scampato dalle ultime epidemiche scoperte.
Passeggerà in un parco nazionale
di unici, di prototipi,
il cane, l'elefante, qualche scheletro
di mammuth e molte mummie di chi fu
l'uomo sapiente, faber, ludens o peggio.

O ipocriti voraci consumate
tutto e voi stessi com'è vostro destino,
ma sia lode al piromane che affretta
ciò che tutti volete con più lento
decorso perché è meglio esser penultimo
che postremo dei vivi! (*Applausi e molte
congratulazioni*).

A Millenarian

Production isn't incremented (*sic*)
by protecting Alma Mater (Alma?).
Tertium non datur; but there *will* be a third—
the only man to escape the most recently identified epidemics.
He'll go strolling in a national park
packed with unique specimens and prototypes—
dog, elephant, some skeletons of mammoths,
and a good many mummies of what was once
Homo sapiens, faber, ludens, or worse.

O, you greedy hypocrites, gobble everything
and yourselves too, as your fate decrees,
but praise to the pyromaniac who hastens
what you all desire but in a longer term
since it's better to be penultimately alive
than the last of living beings! (*Applause and shouts
of congratulation*).

La caduta dei valori

Leggo una tesi di baccalaureato
sulla caduta dei valori.
Chi cade è stato in alto, il che dovevasi
dimostrare, e chi mai fu così folle?

La vita non sta sopra e non sta sotto,
e tanto meno a mezza tacca. Ignora
l'insù e l'ingiù, il pieno e il vuoto, il prima
e il dopo. Del presente non sa un'acca.

Straccia i tuoi fogli, buttali in una fogna,
bacalare di nulla e potrai dire
di essere vivo (forse) per un attimo.

Decline of Values

I'm reading a B.A. thesis
on the decline of values. Logically,
falling implies a height from which
to fall, and who's that stupid?

Life is neither up nor down, and still less
in between. Life has no idea
of up and down, fullness and void, before
and after. And knows zip about the present.

Tear up your pages, ditch them in the sewer,
abandon your degree and you can brag
that you were momentarily alive (maybe).

Il mio ottimismo

Il tuo ottimismo mi dice l'amico
e nemico Benvolio è sconcertante.
Ottimista fu già chi si estasiava
tra i sepolcri inebriandosi del rauco gargarismo
delle strigi;
pessimista colui che con felpati versi
lasciava appena un'orma di pantofola
sul morbido velluto dei giardini inglesi.
Ma tu che godi dell'incenerimento
universale rubi il mestiere ai chierici,
quelli neri s'intende perché i rossi
dormono e mai sarà chi li risvegli.
Ah no, Benvolio, i cherchi ci presentano
un Deus absconditus che ha barba baffi e occhi
a miliardi perché nulla gli sfugge
di noi: e dunque quasi un complice dei nostri
misfatti, un vero onnipotente che
può tutto e non lo può o non lo vuole.
Il mio Artefice no, non è un artificiere
che fa scoppiare tutto, il bene e il male,
e si chiede perché noi ci siamo cacciati
tra i suoi piedi, non chiesti, non voluti,
meno che meno amati. Il mio non è
nulla di tutto questo e perciò lo amo
senza speranza e non gli chiedo nulla.

My Optimism

Your optimism, says my enemy and friend
Benvolio, is disconcerting.
The man who went into raptures amongst sepulchers,
who got drunk on the rasping hoot of screech-owls
was indeed an optimist;
the pessimist was the man of softly muffled verse
whose slippers left scarcely a trace
on the soft velvet of English gardens.
But your relish for universal incineration
cheats clerics of their calling—
the black clerics to be sure, since the reds
are so deep in sleep they'll never waken.
Ah no, Benvolio, the clerics offer us
a *Deus absconditus*, with beard, mustache,
and billions of eyes since nothing of us
escapes him; and who is therefore almost in collusion
with our crimes, a true omnipotent who can accomplish
everything, and who can't, or won't, oblige.
My Artisan, on the other hand, is no artificer who makes
everything, good and evil, explode,
and wonders why we're hounded
between his feet, unsolicited, unwanted,
and loved even less. My Artisan
is none of these things, which is why I love him
desperately and ask nothing of him.

Due epigrammi

I

Non so perché da Dio si pretenda
che punisca le mie malefatte
e premi i miei benefattori. Quello
che Gli compete non è affare nostro.
(Neppure affare Suo probabilmente).
Ciò ch'è orrendo è pensare l'impensabile.

II

Che io debba ricevere il castigo
neppure si discute. Resta oscuro
se ciò accada in futuro oppure ora
o se sia già avvenuto prima ch'io fossi.
Non ch'io intenda evocare l'esecrabile
fantasma del peccato originale.
Il disastro fu prima dell'origine
se un prima e un dopo hanno ancora un senso.

Two Epigrams

I

I don't know why it's held
that God punishes my misdeeds
and rewards my benefactors. What
concerns Him is no business of ours.
(And probably none of His either).
The awful thing is thinking the unthinkable.

II

That I deserve punishment
isn't in dispute. What's unclear
is whether punishment occurs in the future
or now, or took place before I was born.
Not that I mean to evoke the cursed
spectre of original sin.
The disaster preceded the origin—
if before and after still have any meaning.

Diamantina

Poiché l'ipotisposi di un'arcana
Deità posta a guardia degli scrigni
dei sommi Mercuriali non si addice
a te, Adelheit, apparsa come può
tra zaffate di Averno baluginare
una Fenice che mai seppe aedo
idoleggiare,
così conviene che io mi arresti e muti
la mia protasi in facile discorso.

Si trattava soltanto di sorvolare
o sornuotare qualche eventuale specchio
di pozzanghera e dopo col soccorso
di sbrecciati scalini la scoperta
che il mondo dei cristalli ha i suoi rifugi.
C'è un tutto che si sgretola e qualcosa
che si sfaccetta. Tra i due ordini
l'alternarsi o lo scambio non può darsi.
Forse un cristallo non l'hai veduto mai,
né un vaso di Pandora né un Niagara
di zaffiri. Ma c'era la tua immagine
non ipotiposizzabile, per sua natura,
anzi sfuggente, libera e sfaccettata
fino all'estremo limite, pulviscolare.
Ma il mio errore mi è caro, dilettissima
alunna di un artifice che mai
poté sbalzarti nelle sue medaglie.
Era appena la Vita, qualche cosa
che tutti supponiamo senza averne le prove,

Diamantina

Since the hypothesis of an arcane Divinity
dispatched to protect the strongboxes of the supreme
Mercurials has no appeal for you, Adelheit—
a Phoenix no Greek bard could idolize,
making his epiphany amongst Avernus' belching flames—
it is fitting that I desist, and let my protasis
shift to simple discourse.

It was only a matter of flying or swimming
across a few potential mirrors
of slimy pools and later, with the help
of broken rungs, the discovery
that the world of crystals has its places of refuge.
There is a whole that crumbles, and something else,
a faceted thing. Between these two orders
there can be no alternation, no commerce.
Perhaps you have never seen a crystal,
or a Pandora's box, or a Niagara
of sapphires. But *there* was your image,
by nature incapable of being hypothesized;
on the contrary, elusive, free, faceted
to the utmost limit, pulverized.
But my blunder is dear to me, darling
student of an artifice which could never mint
your image in its medallions.
It was hardly Life, a thing
we all postulate without the slightest proof,

la vita di cui siamo testimoni
noi tutti, non di parte, non di accusa,
non di difesa ma che tu conosci
anche soltanto con le dita
quando sfiori un oggetto che ti dica io e te
siamo UNO.

that life of which we are all witnesses,
not partisans, not prosecutors,
nor defenders, but which you recognize
merely by the touch of your fingers
when you graze an object that tells you
you and I are ONE.

Si deve preferire
la ruga al liscio.
Questo pensava
un uomo tra gli scogli
molti anni fa.
Ma avvenne dopo
che tutto fu corrugato
e da allora l'imbroglio
non fu più sbrogliato.
Non più dunque un problema
quello di preferire
ma piuttosto
di essere preferiti.
Ma neppure questione
perché non c'entra la volontà.
Essa vuole soltanto
differire
e differire non è indifferenza.
Questa è soltanto degli Dei,
non certo
dell'uomo tra gli scogli.

We must prefer
the wrinkled to the smooth.
Many years ago
this was the thought
of a man on the horns of a dilemma.
But later it came about
that everything was wrinkled
and from then on the muddle
never got untangled.
Therefore the problem
was no longer one of preferring
but rather
of being preferred.
But it's not even a question
since the will is not involved.
It wants only
to differ
and differing isn't indifference.
Indifference is only for Gods,
clearly not
for a man on the horns of a dilemma.

Non partita di boxe o di ramino
tra i due opposti Luciferi o eventuali
postumi tirapiedi dei medesimi.
Non può darsi sconfitto o vincitore
senza conflitto e di ciò i gemelli
non hanno alcun sentore. Ognuno crede di essere
l'Unico, quello che non trova ostacoli
sul suo cammino.

No boxing match or card-game
between two opposed Lucifers or possible
posthumous stooges of the same.
Without a struggle neither one
can win or lose, a fact of which the twins
haven't an inkling. Each thinks
he's the One, that the right-of-way
is exclusively his.

Sorapis, 40 anni fa

Non ho amato mai molto la montagna
e detesto le Alpi. Le Ande, le Cordigliere
non le ho vedute mai. Pure la Sierra
de Guadarrama mi ha rapito, dolce
com'è l'ascesa e in vetta daini, cervi
secondo le notizie dei dépliants turistici.
Solo l'elettrica aria dell'Engadina
ci vinse, mio insettino, ma non si era
tanto ricchi da dirci hic manebimus.
Tra i laghi solo quello di Sorapis
fu la grande scoperta. C'era la solitudine
delle marmotte più udite che intraviste
e l'aria dei Celesti; ma quale strada
per accedervi? Dapprima la percorsi
da solo per vedere se i tuoi occhietti
potevano addentrarsi tra cunicoli
zigzaganti tra lastre alte di ghiaccio.
E così lunga! Confortata solo
nel primo tratto, in folti di conifere,
dallo squillo d'allarme delle ghiandaie.
Poi ti guidai tenendoti per mano
fino alla cima, una capanna vuota.
Fu quello il nostro lago, poche spanne d'acqua,
due vite troppo giovani per essere vecchie,
e troppo vecchie per sentirsi giovani.
Scoprimmo allora che cos'è l'età.
Non ha nulla a che fare col tempo, è qualcosa che dice
che ci fa dire siamo qui, è un miracolo
che non si può ripetere. Al confronto
la gioventù è il più vile degl'inganni.

Sorapis, 40 Years Ago

I've never been very fond of mountains
and I detest the Alps. I've never seen the Andes
or the Cordilleras. But I found the Sierra
de Guadarrama ravishing, with its gentle
ascent and fallow deer and stags on the peaks
as pictured in the tourist brochures.
Only the electric air of the Engadine
won us over, dear Mosca, but it wasn't
so richly rewarding that we said, *hic manebimus.*
Among lakes, our only great find was Sorapis.
It had the solitude of marmots, more often
heard than seen, and the air of the Celestials;
but the road that took you there! At first
I traveled it alone to see if your eyes
could penetrate the clouds zigzagging
through lofty slabs of ice. And such a
long journey! The only solace in the first stretch,
through dense conifers, was the alarmed screeching
of the jays. Then I took you by the hand
and led you to the summit and an abandoned hut.
It was our lake, its waters a few spans wide,
and we were two lives too young to be old,
and too old to feel young.
Then we discovered what aging is.
It has nothing to do with time, it's something
that makes us say we're here, a miracle
that happens only once. By comparison,
youth is the vilest of illusions.

Senza colpi di scena

Le stagioni
sono quasi scomparse.
Era tutto un inganno degli Spiriti
dell'Etere.

Non si può essere vivi
a momenti, a sussulti, a scappa e fuggi
lunghi o brevi.

O si è vivi o si è morti, l'altalena
non poteva durare oltre l'eterna
fugacissima età della puerizia.

Ora comincia il ciclo della stagnazione.
Le stagioni si sono accomiatate
senza salamelecchi o cerimonie, stanche
dei loro turni. Non saremo più
tristi o felici, uccelli d'alba o notturni.
Non sapremo nemmeno
che sia sapere e non sapere, vivere
o quasi o nulla affatto. È presto detto,
il resto lo vedremo a cose fatte.

No Coups de théâtre

The seasons
have almost vanished.
It was all an illusion of the Ethereal
Spirits.

You can't be alive
momentarily, by starts, wild stampedings,
long or short.

You're alive or you're dead, the swing
couldn't last beyond the fleeting
eternity of childhood.

Now the cycle of stagnation begins.
The seasons, weary of revolving,
have taken their leave with no ceremonial
bowing and scraping. We'll no longer be
sad or happy, dawn-birds or nocturnals.
We won't even know
what it is to know and not to know, to live,
or almost live, or not at all. In a word,
we'll see what happens after the fact.

In hoc signo . . .

A Roma un'agenzia di pompe funebri
si chiama L'AVVENIRE. E poi si dice
che l'umor nero è morto con Jean Paul,
Gionata Swift e Achille Campanile.

In hoc signo . . .

At Rome there's a funeral agency called
THE FUTURE. And they say
black humor died with Jean Paul,
Swift, and Achille Campanili!

L'élan vital

Fu quando si concesse il dottorato
honoris causa a tale Lamerdière di Friburgo,
se Svizzera o Brisgovia per me è lo stesso.
Salì sul podio avvolto da sciarpame
onnicolore e vomitò il suo Obiurgo.
Depreco disse il bruco e la connessa
angelica farfalla che n'esce per estinguersi
con soffio di fiammifero svedese.
Aborro ciò ch'è tenue, silenzioso,
evanescente. Non c'è altro dio che il Rombo,
non il pesce ma il tuono universale
ininterrotto, l'antiteleologico.
Non il bisbiglio che i sofisti dicono
l'élan vital. Se dio è parola e questa
è suono, tale immane bombo
che non ha inizio né avrà fine è il solo
obietto che è se stesso e tutto l'altro.
Muore Giove, Eccellenze, e l'inno del Poeta
NON resta. A tale punto
un Jumbo ruppe le mie orecchie ed io
fui desto.

L'Élan Vital

It happened when a doctorate *honoris causa*
was awarded to a certain Lamerdière of Freiburg—
Switzerland or Breisgau, who cares?
Garbed in rainbow gown, he mounted
the dais and barfed his Objurgation.
I revile the larva, he said, the grub from which,
in due course, issues the angelic butterfly
only to die in the flaring of a match.
I despise the silent, the tenuous,
the fading. The only god is Rhombus,
not the mullet, but the everlasting anti-
teleological, universal thunderclap.
Not that susurrus which sophists call
l'élan vital. If god is word,
and word is sound, this almighty bombination,
for which no beginning is, no end will ever be,
is unique in being both itself and everything else.
Jove dies, your Excellencies, the poet's hymn
does NOT last. At this point a Jumbo
jet blasted my ears
and I woke.

La danzatrice stanca

Torna a fiorir la rosa
che pur dianzi languia . . .

Dianzi? Vuol dir dapprima, poco fa.
E quando mai può dirsi per stagioni
che s'incastrano l'una nell'altra, amorfe?
Ma si parlava della rifioritura
d'una convalescente, di una guancia
meno pallente ove non sia muffito
l'aggettivo, del più vivido accendersi
dell'occhio, anzi del guardo.
È questo il solo fiore che rimane
con qualche merto d'un tuo Dulcamara.
A te bastano i piedi sulla bilancia
per misurare i pochi milligrammi
che i già defunti turni stagionali
non seppero sottrarti. Poi potrai
rimettere le ali non più nubecola
celeste ma terrestre e non è detto
che il cielo se ne accorga. Basta che uno
stupisca che il tuo fiore si rincarna
a meraviglia. Non è di tutti i giorni
in questi nivei défilés di morte.

Tired Dancer

"The rose that lately languished
now comes blooming back . . ."

Lately? It means "recently," "just now."
And how can that be said of seasons that fit,
indistinguishably, inside one another?
But the lines concerned a convalescent's
recovery of health, a cheek
less pallid where the adjective doesn't mean
sickly, and a livelier fire
in the eye, even in the gaze.
This is the sole bloom remaining
with some of the merits of your various Dulcamaras.
Feet on the scale, you're happy,
measuring the few milligrams
which the now defunct turning of the seasons
could not subtract. Later you'll be able
to put on wings again, tiny celestial clouds
no longer, but earthly ones, of which the sky is said
to take no notice. Enough that someone does,
amazed by the miracle that makes your body
bloom again. Not an everyday event
in these snowy *défilés* of death.

Al mio grillo

Che direbbe il mio grillo
dice la Gina osservando il merlo
che becca larve e bruchi dentro i vasi
da fiori del balcone e fa un disastro.
Ma il più bello è che il grillo eri tu
finché vivesti e lo sapemmo in pochi.
Tu senza occhietti a spillo di cui porto
un doppio, un vero insetto di celluloide
con due palline che sarebbero gli occhi,
due pistilli e ci guarda da un canterano.
Che ne direbbe il grillo d'allora del suo sosia
e del merlo? È per lei che sono qui
dice la Gina e scaccia con la scopa il merlaccio.
Poi s'alzano le prime saracinesche. È giorno.

To My Cricket

What would my cricket say,
says Gina, watching the blackbird
calamitously pecking at larva and grubs
in the big flowerpots on the balcony.
But the funny thing is that the cricket was you
when you were alive. We saw it in little things.
It was you, minus those piercing eyes whose double
I wear, a real celluloid insect
with two little beads in place of eyes,
two pistils, looking at us from a bureau.
What would the former cricket say of her double
and the blackbird? You're the reason I'm here,
says Gina, chasing off the blackbird with her broom.
Then the first blinds go up. It's day.

Per finire

Raccomando ai miei posteri
(se ne saranno) in sede letteraria,
il che resta improbabile, di fare
un bel falò di tutto che riguardi
la mia vita, i miei fatti, i miei nonfatti.
Non sono un Leopardi, lascio poco da ardere
ed è già troppo vivere in percentuale.
Vissi al cinque per cento, non aumentate
la dose. Troppo spesso invece piove
sul bagnato.

In Conclusion

I charge my posterity
(if any) in the domain of literature,
which is quite unlikely, to make
a huge bonfire of everything
relating to my life, my actions
and non-actions. I'm no Leopardi,
I leave little to the fire,
and it's already too much to live
on percentages. I did my living
at the rate of five percent; don't increase
the dose. It never rains
but it pours.

Notes

Poetic Diary: 1971

To Leone Traverso

Leone Traverso (1910–1968) was a philologist, classicist, scholar of German literature, and translator, especially of Rilke and of Greek tragedy. He represents for E.M. an ideal of literary devotion to a great tradition (including the Provençal troubadours). The phrase *mestre de gay saber* is Catalan for the medieval Provençal expression meaning a master of the "gay science," the art of poetry. Nietzsche, of course, used it as the title of his book, *The Gay Science*. The Catalan poet and politician Victor Balaguer (1824–1901) was proclaimed *mestre de gay saber* in 1861. E.M. contrasts his own disenchantment to Traverso's idealism and the rich, multilingual, European culture he embodied.

Like Zaccheus

Alas, I'm no treecreeper: Zaccheus, the tax collector who climbed a sycamore tree to see Jesus pass by, and whose house Jesus elected to visit, to the shock of his disciples. Luke: 19.

To C.

C: Clizia (Irma Brandeis).

a feeder of birds: For the Italian *imbeccatore*. The verb *imbeccare* means to feed young birds and, figuratively, to put words in someone's mouth, to prompt. An *imbeccatore* can either be a feeder of birds or a prompter in the theater. E.M.'s French translator, Patrice Angelini, opts for prompter, translating *nicchia / dell'imbeccatore* as *le trou du souffleur* (Eugenio Montale, *Carnets de poésie 1971 et 1972, poèmes épars*, tr. Patrice Angelini [*Nouvelle revue française*, Gallimard: 1979], pp. 29, 251). W.A. defended his choice of "feeder of birds" on the grounds that E.M. was obsessed with birds and wrote of them often. However, the variant recorded in *Eugenio Montale, L'opera in versi*, edited by Rosanna Bettarini and Gianfranco Contini (Turin: 1980), gives evidence in favor of the prompter. E.M.'s early draft had the word *suggeritore* for *imbeccatore*, and indicates the theatrical prompter, at least in an earlier phase of the poet's thinking. In the later version, E.M. would have enjoyed the ornithological play on words, which may indeed have "prompted" his revision.

El Desdichado

El Desdichado: In Spanish, "the unfortunate, the ill-starred," the title of a famous sonnet by Gérard de Nerval (1808–1855), whose second line Eliot incorporated into the end of *The Waste Land* (*"Le Prince d'Aquitaine à la tour abolie"*). Nerval, a suicide, profoundly influenced French Symbolist and, later, Surrealist poetry. E.M. called him "one of the most inspired of the French poets," and wrote: "The two coins found in his pocket, his crises of madness, thus explain Nerval's end; or was it rather his haste to regain the nameless country from which Gérard, *el desdichado*, the forsaken, felt himself exiled?" (Ricci, 75).

Where Charity Begins

Malvolio: The character of the over-reaching, ambitious, and delusional steward in Shakespeare's *Twelfth Night, or What You Will*. In E.M.'s poem, he is a mask for Pier Paolo Pasolini, who had attacked *Satura* in *Nuovi argomenti*, No. 21, 1971, pp. 17–20. Malvolio appears in one other poem of E.M.'s addressed to Pasolini: "Letter to Malvolio" in *Poetic Diary: 1971*. Many critics also see Pasolini in the figure of Benvolio in "The Horse" and "My Optimism" in *Poetic Diary: 1972*: E.M. played coy about these identifications. In one interview he said of Malvolio, "He's not a specific person, and he's even less the Shakespearian character of that name." In another interview, he said of Pasolini: "It's he who recognized himself [in Malvolio], publishing insolences in *Nuovi argomenti*. I never said so." (Ricci, 177).

The Triumph of Trash

a Chantal, suddenly blowing in from the north: A young woman named Adelaide Bellingardi to whom the elder poet became attached. Under the name of Adelheit she appears in *Poetic Diary: 1972* in "Diamantina"; in "Harmony" in *Poetic Diary: 1972*; and again in "Agile messenger here you are" in *Posthumous Diary* translated by Jonathan Galassi (New York: Turtle Point Press, 2001). In a note to "Diamantina" in *L'Opera in versi* (Torino: Einaudi, 1980), 1101, E.M. writes: "It's a variation on a theme already developed in 'The Triumph of Trash' [in *Poetic Diary: 1971*]. Only the character has changed names" (from Chantal to Adelheit).

The Imponderable

Filli: Phyllis, another one of E.M.'s mythologized women. As "Filli," she turns up in several different guises in E.M.'s prose: in "Gli occhi limpidi" in

Farfalla di Dinard ("Miss Filli Parkinson, the restorer who breathed life back into some old crusts in the Laroche collection"), and as quite a different person in the prose sketch "Farfalla di Dinard" ("the graceful Filli," a waitress in the café in the piazza of Dinard). (Ricci, 159). Phyllis was a Thracian princess who fell in love with Demophon, son of Theseus, when he stopped in Thrace on his way back from the Trojan War. As recounted in Ovid's *Heroides* II, Demophon abandoned her, though promising to return. Despairing, Phyllis hanged herself, and in her bitterness was transformed into an almond tree. Phyllis also appears in Dante, *Paradiso* IX, 100–102, as an example of a suffering lover in the sphere of Venus. E.M.'s poem is both heavy and light: Phyllis is a conventional name for a pastoral maiden, lighthearted and erotically available (as in Virgil's Eclogue III); as the Thracian princess, she is associated with suicide by hanging. E.M. plays on both. In this poem, it is the male speaker who is heavy and who contemplates hanging himself.

Letter to Bobi

Bobi Bazlen (1902–1965) was an erudite writer and translator of German from Trieste. He was one of E.M.'s oldest and dearest friends; it was he, early on, who introduced the poet to Italo Svevo and his novels, then almost unknown. Bazlen brought the works of Freud, Kafka, and Musil into Italy, and worked as an adviser to influential publishing houses, including Bompiani, Einaudi, and Adelphi, which he helped to found. His own writings were collected and published posthumously by Roberto Calasso. In an article in the *Corriere della sera* in 1969, E.M. wrote of Bazlen: "He wouldn't have liked to be called a man of letters, a writer, an intellectual, or any other such moniker; suspicious as he was of any mysticism, he would laugh if I defined him as a mystic of anonymity. It's certain that he spent his life in the desire not to leave any tangible trace of his passage." (Ricci, 165).

Stimmung: German for mood, atmosphere. In his 1969 article on Bazlen, E.M. wrote: "When I knew him, he insisted outright that our language, deprived of *Stimmung* and of interiority, could never produce anything worthwhile. . . ." (Ricci, 165). See the classic discussion of *Stimmung* in Leo Spitzer, *Classical and Christian Ideas of World Harmony*, ed. Anna Granville Hatcher (Baltimore: Johns Hopkins University Press, 1963).

Without Surprise

these Sunday transhumances: Transhumance means the seasonal moving of herds up to and down from the mountain pastures. But perhaps E.M. is allowing here an ironic and distorted echo of Dante's phrase, *trashumanar significa per verba / non si poria* from *Paradiso* I, 67–69: "to transcend the human cannot be described in words." No transcendental experience disturbs the crowds in E.M.'s poem.

Letter to Malvolio

Malvolio: As in "Where Charity Begins," a mask for Pier Paolo Pasolini. See note for "Where Charity Begins."

my taking flight: Pasolini accused E.M. of bourgeois cynicism and narcissism, and claimed E.M. had "liberated" himself from Marxism, but not from power and privilege.

But later when the stables had emptied: See "Thrust and Parry, I" in *Satura*, where E.M. describes Italy under Fascism as the Augean stables, overwhelmed with manure.

phocomele: A monstrous birth defect in which the arms and legs are so shortened that the hands and feet seem to grow directly from the body's trunk.

since you know that tomorrow will be impossible: Pasolini had stated, "Marxism believes in *time* and its literary critics believe in *times*; science [according to E.M.] shows that they are mistaken . . . ; that everything returns, or stays the same, at any rate, there's no such thing as 'progress.' Therefore if Marxism is an unsustainable illusion, E.M. liberates himself from Marxism. . . ."

p.p.c.

p.p.c.: conventional formula for a closing salutation, *per prendere congedo*, to take one's leave. E.M. elliptically takes his leave of this volume of poems, and imagines taking leave of his life.

Chiliasts: Millenarian Christians who believed that Christ would establish a Golden Age on earth for a thousand years before the End of the World.

Poetic Diary: 1972

The Odor of Heresy

miss Petrus: D. Petrus, author of *Autobiography and Life of George Tyrrell*.

the Barnabite: E.M. attended a high school in Genoa run by Barnabite priests, and was particularly influenced by his elder sister Marianna's philosophy teacher, Padre Giuseppe Trinchero (1875–1936), a freethinking Barnabite priest who visited the family on Sundays and with whom the young E.M. took long walks, plunged in philosophical and literary conversation.

The Horse

Caracalla's horse: Caracalla (186–217) was one of the most brutal of the Roman emperors. But it was the emperor Caligula (12–41) who expressed his contempt for the Roman Senate by threatening to make his horse a consul. E.M. was made senator for life in 1967.

Benvolio: Originally written "Malvolio" in manuscript versions; see *L'Opera in versi*, 1084. Benvolio is Romeo's friend and cousin in Shakespeare's *The Tragedy of Romeo and Juliet*. Often taken as another mask for Pasolini; see notes to "Where Charity Begins" and "Letter to Malvolio." Of the double identity of Pasolini as Malvolio-Benvolio, Ricci writes that "rather than a different character, they are now different ideological aspects referring to the same figure: if not precisely to Pasolini, at least to the same image of a falsely *engagé* intellectual (according to Montale)." (Ricci, 228).

To a Great Philosopher

a Great Philosopher: Benedetto Croce (1866–1952), the major Italian philosopher of the twentieth century. Croce was an Idealist, and placed aesthetics at the center of philosophical inquiry. He was also a prominent political liberal and anti-Fascist. E.M. met Croce four times. Some of E.M.'s essential philosophical vocabulary (especially the concept of Immanence) derives from Croce; in the Imaginary Interview in 1946 the poet writes: "Later I preferred Croce's great Idealistic positivism. . . ." (Forti, 80). E.M. both chides and salutes Croce in this poem. E.M. also wrote of Croce: "There's something obscure in the margins of his thought, something resembling the Stoic faith. It's this shadow, more than anything else, that connects us to Croce and makes us feel him as still present. . . . More even than his aesthetics . . . it's his call for moral responsibility, for 'paying with one's own person,' that, beyond any political or religious conviction, makes us feel the force of his presence today." (Ricci, 272).

In an "Italian" Garden

General Pelloux: Luigi Pelloux (1839–1924), military general and politician. Chief of General Staff in the Italian Army in 1896; Minister of War in two cabinets.

The New Iconographers

While Olympic ensigns flutter on the pennants: In September 1972, the members of the Palestinian group Black September kidnapped and then killed eleven members of the Israeli Olympic team at the Summer Olympics in Munich.

Annetta

Annetta: A key figure who haunts E.M.'s poetry, early and late. Arletta, or Annetta, was a friend from childhood who died young, and represents a mythic, adolescent eroticism. In *Cuttlefish Bones* she appears in "Wind and Banners" and "Shoot stretching from the wall . . ."

in the section *Other Verses*, in "Delta," and in "Encounter." In *The Occasions* she appears in "The Balcony" and "The Coastguard Station"; in *The Storm and Other Things* in "Two in Twilight." See note to "Encounter" in *Cuttlefish Bones.*

Opinions

Calpurnius: A Roman bucolic poet who lived in the time of Nero. He seems to be a stand-in for E.M. in his almost nihilistic mode: "But no, says Calpurnius. Life is hardly a sound . . ."

A Millenarian

A Millenarian: A Chiliast, a believer that Christ will appear and establish a reign of a thousand years of happiness on earth. That is, a believer in a fantasy of progress and achieved felicity, but also someone who looks forward fervently to the end of the world. See "p.p.c" at the end of *Poetic Diary: 1971*. In his Nobel Prize acceptance speech, E.M. reflected on the post-war feverish consumerism and debasement of culture, and declared: "It's a remarkable fact that a kind of general millenarianism accompanies an ever more widely spread 'comfort,' that well-being (where it exists, that is in limited spaces on the earth) should have the livid marks of despair." (Forti, 92).

My Optimism

Benvolio: See note to "The Horse."

Diamantina

Adelheit: An old-fashioned (medieval) woman's name in German, with overtones of nobility. E.M. thus idealized the young woman Adelaide Bellingardi whom he had met in Rome where she worked for the jeweler Bulgari; her association with gems gives rise to the conceit of this poem, the opposition of immortal, diamantine beauty and the "elusive, free" life force admired in the young woman. She appears as Chantal in "The Triumph of Trash" in *Poetic Diary: 1971*, and as Adelheit in "Harmony" in *Poetic Notebook (1974–77)* as well as in "Agile messenger here you are" in *Posthumous Diary*. See note to "The Triumph of Trash."

Sorapis, 40 Years Ago

Sorapis: A lake in the Dolomites. In her comment on this poem Ricci quotes E.M.'s article on the Engadine region in the mountains of southern Switzerland and Northern Italy from the *Corriere della sera* in 1949: ". . . here, in this lacustrine plateau at two thousand feet above sea level, in this Eden protected on all sides, barely accessible, dominated by high peaks, ideal for long mountain hikes and at the same time conducive to long, indolent inertias . . . ; here one can truly breathe life, letting every other bond fall away and forgetting even one's own historical, concrete, and predetermined mask." (Ricci, 373–74).

Tired Dancer

"The rose that lately languished now comes blooming back . . .": From Giuseppe Parini's poem "La educazione," 1764. Parini was an eminent neoclassical Italian poet (1729–1799).

To My Cricket

Gina: Gina Tiossi, E.M.'s housekeeper in his later years. She assumes the role of female guardian; see "The Swift" in *Poetic Diary: 1971*, and "All Souls' Day" and "Notes" in *Poetic Notebook 1974–1977*.

the cricket was you: Once again, E.M. remembers Mosca, this time imagined not as a fly, but as a cricket.

Index

Index

Index